Moral Meltdown

The Core of Globalism

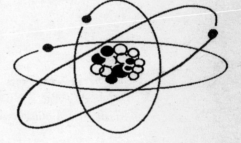

by
Hilmar von Campe

Prescott Press, Inc.

Prescott Press
P.O. Box 53788
Lafayette, Louisiana 70505

Library of Congress Card Catalog Number 95-072814
ISBN 0-933451-35-0

Printed in the U.S.A.

Contents

iii

nation. What I believe to be a satisfactory and comprehensive explanation can be found on the following pages. What I have written about is not simply an intellectual explanation of things past. Rather, it is a direct challenge to the present-day human existence of every individual and to the actions of every politically responsible leader, without regard to country, continent, or color.

A decisive issue is what governments are for: what ethical standards their actions are guided by, and what information their actions are based on. As a matter of fact, there is no difference whatsoever for the individual who is held to precisely the same issues. Governments are the representatives of personal and national self-interests, the latter being by and large nothing less than the multiplication of the selfishness of millions of individuals who manage to give it a positive-sounding, patriotic name. The difference between nations is only the spectrum of what is understood in one's own interests. We have not even started to understand the truth about ourselves, the illogical and contradictory nature of our actions which appear normal to us (e.g., that Christian people who pray to the same God for victory and protection are slaughtering one another, as was the case in Europe during the First World War). This involved the slaughtering of so-called heathen people from other continents. First suppressing and then attempting to convert them to our faith and civilization doesn't appear as a contradiction to the beliefs we profess, yet those around us indeed see the contradiction.

My uncle was the first German ambassador to Chile after World War II. He was a good and respected ambassador, and part of his function was to re-create a positive German image abroad. He had a limited set of contacts to draw his information from, primarily government people, the cocktail circuit, and the major newspapers. On my visits to Chile, my uncle introduced me to many of his contacts within and outside the government. Within a few days I had talked to not only my uncle's contacts, but to the students at the universities, to the workers and trade union people, to the disgruntled intellectuals, to the poor inhabitants of the colonies, and to the housewives as well. Soon I knew more about the real situation of the country than the entire embassy as a whole.

In the hearings regarding Robert Gates' nomination for the position of director of the Central Intelligence Agency, failures in the reporting on Mexico were pointed out. These failures led to embarrassing political consequences. I know Mexico quite well. I lived there and operated my automotive parts factory for fourteen years. A few years ago I had lunch with a member of the American Embassy. He was the charge d'affaires at that time, if I remember correctly. He told me that the embassy was basically concerned with the economic situation and was closely following the related developments. Since my wife and I were running our two businesses, a factory and a travel agency which provided for our living (we were also active members of the German and American Chambers of Commerce), I was naturally always on top of the important economic events. I was also in daily contact with my workers and employees and, as a businessman, I was exposed to the pattern of behavior of the government bureaucracy. I was circulating among Mexicans of all backgrounds and could well distinguish between government declarations and reality. I believe that Robert Gates, or his successors, would gain a substantially more solid political picture from me than from his staff.

I know of two Western intelligence services that have gone through the facts and figures given in this book and are keenly interested in how I gather my information and what opinions I hold on various situations. Apart from collecting information, one must know what to do with it. The interpretation of the information depends on the value system being applied and the objectives being pursued—this is how conclusions are reached.

An intelligence officer, for example, who looked at the Soviet Union and thought that the most important issue was the military threat and concentrated on that, may have gathered important and necessary facts, but would have missed the boat by far. In my analysis of 1988 (published in Germany in 1989), quite a number of things I said then were substantiated by the developments, though I admit that the speed of events took me by surprise. In addition to what I said above, I have a clear value system, which is explained in this book. I use my value system in deciding what I think is important and what is not. This allows me to go straight to the heart of issues, to see through the outside clamor, and to drop the superficial side aspects to find out what really makes people and leaders tick. I therefore do not just speak of individual events in different countries but of the system of individual and government action, the system of self-deceit. This system of self-deceit causes individuals and governments to repeat the same mistakes and perpetuate the same misjudgments over decades and through centuries, causing them to go nowhere. So I put forward what I consider the only viable solution for mankind.

According to a 1991 NBC poll, 70 percent of Americans feel that they, and their country, are off track and have lost their destiny. According to this survey, no one really had a clue as to precisely what was wrong, how to tackle the problem, or where to start doing something about it. The war in the Middle East, with its so-called victory, was initially lifting morale and bringing back a strong sense of patriotism, but the unsatisfactory end left the confusion intact. It is time for the world's leading power to get its act together. Maybe it is embarrassing for an American to hear a foreigner talk about the destiny of America. But, as a father and a brother of American citizens, I am in the core of my being as little a foreigner to America as I am to Peru, the home-land of my wife; to Mexico, where I lived and worked for so long; or to Chile, which I have taken into my heart since I arrived in Latin America in the fifties. I get upset when I see what the Chinese rulers, with our help, do to their people and to the Tibetans. I worry about developments in South Africa, and I get worried when I watch the deterioration of the spiritual and moral conditions of my own country, Germany, which my forefathers served. The defeat and moral destruction of the Nazi years has deeply hurt me. I shall always be a German who cherishes his own tradition, but I am as committed to the well-being of other nations and their people as I am committed to my own country and to my compatriots. And so I am committed to America, the moral decline of which I find exasperating, and to my American friends, whose battle for truth I want to reinforce.

I view my book as a massive frontal attack on hypocrisy, sanctimonious news, and self-righteousness; in short, the lie that has taken over our society. The spirit of our times is the spirit of moral neutrality that, with scintillating reasoning, tempts us to look for our own interests on the path of least resistance. This adaptation to the spirit of the times—manifesting itself in various ways in different cultural, social, and political structures—is called opportunism.

Opportunism is the consequence of the lack of an overriding purpose bigger than oneself and one's nation. This is what I see as the basic evil that can be found at the root of all economic and political problems. In the end, condoning evil in one's own life leads to condoning evil in society and to the appeasement of totalitarian systems. It is moral defeat in the lives of politicians that leads to political concepts of appeasement. Moral change will lead to political change.

The false moral structures and intellectual concepts that are created out of injustice and evil have to be destroyed. We have to break through the mental limitations that constrain us and delude us into thinking that if so many people are doing it, it must therefore be right. Adapting to the spirit of the time is not tantamount to consciously doing evil, but going with the pack can easily wash you into the abyss. The murky bowl of lies covering our world can only be destroyed with the hammer of truth.

Today, what especially attracts our attention are the fast-paced technological advances and the increasing affluence of a few. Those involved see this as a never-ending boom, leading many to feel like gods. It is my opinion that the boom will quickly come to a horrible end if the foundations of our society are not put in order. I am of the greatest conviction that we have the strength to create a different world in which God rules.

To make this happen, the people of the truth (you and I) have to grasp the initiative and go on the offensive throughout the world. This book is an attempt to show how and why.

Acknowledgments

I am grateful to my sister, Sibylle, and my brother-in-law, Hans Heidrich, who worked long evenings over the first draft of my manuscript and always backed me up; and to Dr. Craig W. Nickisch, John Christman, Kathlin Razi, and Rev. Bill Price, who read and corrected the draft manuscript or parts of it in its various phases. I also thank Javier Mazetti for helping me to get my manuscript in presentable form. The faith and support of my wife Dina were a constant source of encouragement and inspiration for this volume. She never complained when I spent our money on my investigations and disappeared, sometimes for weeks, into the various corners of the world.

I am also grateful to my Mexican employees and workers, whose faithfulness kept our factory operation on-line during my many absences.

Finally, I want to thank John Hargreaves, who was instrumental in making this book a reality.

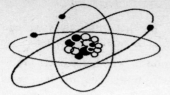

Objectives

Each of us has objectives which determine our actions: buying a new car, getting promoted, building a house, taking the family to Florida, establishing one's own business—or whatever. For most people, though, objectives are a purely personal matter and limited to one's own life. They are not embedded into more far-reaching objectives like serving one's country, obeying God, or changing society. Very often an individual starts out with a passion to serve his country and ends up only fighting for his career. A society that is composed mainly of people who seek only their personal objectives is in grave danger of disintegrating, especially if the leadership has the same motive and does not lift up and motivate society (as it should by definition of leadership). People all around the world normally respond to leaders who set objectives for the whole of society. Unfortunately, people will also follow objectives at times when they might not be in the best interest of the country, as the Germans did under the Nazis.

The lack of objectives in Western societies could be disguised in the last decades by what might be described as "Cold War" activities. That sort of policy, of course, was nothing else but a reaction to what the other so-called cold warrior did, and was normally accompanied by indignation and declarations of our own Western goodness and righteousness. We have convinced ourselves now that there is less to react to. This is because the Soviet military threat is diminishing for lack of money. Now we appear naked because we do not have objectives we can define and rally behind (apart from trying to get richer). To those who look beyond the question of whether Robert Gates knew anything about the diversion of funds from the Iran arms sale to the Nicaraguan Contras, that point became very clear in the confirmation hearings of the Senate Intelligence Committee in September 1991. I was impressed with those men because they seemed to be able to rise above partisanship. At the same time, I doubt that any of the senators could articulate the overriding goals of America and Western society. This is necessary to stay in the context of the hearing, so as to direct the intelligence community as to what to look for in other countries and to know how to evaluate the information the government then receives. The less there is of an overriding national purpose and objectives for society on which the various factions of a country (and an alliance of countries, for that matter) can agree, the more divergence exists between those factions. This results in vastly different conceptions of priorities, and heavy infighting breaks out to determine what should be done and how the available money should be spent. Some say that the strength of democracy is to accommodate many different opinions. That may be true in some cases, but what meets the eye now is constant bickering on issues in the absence of an overriding common purpose. "You have to operate in the jungle of democracy," said one senator to Gates, "and [you] are being caught in the cat and mouse play between Congress and the White House."

The call has gone out to determine the "new priorities after the Cold War." This will be very difficult for a nation and a society without purpose because priorities can only be defined according to the objectives. Maybe we can learn something from totalitarian leaders. In his book entitled *My Break with Moscow*, Arkady N. Shevchenko tells how he once asked the then-Soviet foreign minister, Andrei Gromyko, to define the greatest weakness of American foreign policy. Gromyko answered: "They don't comprehend our final goals. And they mistake tactics for strategy. Besides, they have too many doctrines and concepts proclaimed at different times; but the absence of a solid, coherent and consistent policy is their big flaw."[1]

John Reston once asked Pres. John F. Kennedy how he
imagined the world should be and what vision he had of the
future. Ralph G. Martin, the biographer and author, quotes
Kennedy's reply: "I have not yet had time to think about it."[2]
There could scarcely be any clearer expression of the aimlessness
of Western leaders and societies. Kennedy was a virtuoso in
controlling the political machinery of the U.S. and he delivered
the most moving speeches. Countless Americans voted for him,
fascinated by the personality of this representative of a new
generation of political leaders. But neither they nor the president of the strongest nation in the free world had the slightest
idea where mankind should be heading. Unlike Europe, America
does have a global policy, but it lacks a concept and a policy for
mankind.

When Kennedy accepted his nomination as the Democrats'
presidential candidate before an audience of eighty thousand in
the Los Angeles Colosseum, his speech was loaded with expressions such as "new frontier," "challenge," "undiscovered areas of
science and space exploration," and "war and peace," which
brought him the same thunderous applause as Joseph Goebbels
was accustomed to receiving in the Berlin Sports Palace. "Fantastic," commented a spectator. "But what does it all mean?"
Goebbels had a clearer idea than Kennedy of the future he
envisaged for the world.

Listening to the dozen or so U.S. presidential candidates in
the late eighties and early nineties, one is unfortunately forced
to conclude that their ideas are even less adequate than Kennedy's.
Neither the Americans nor the Europeans—to say nothing of
governments in other parts of the world—have any long-term
global objectives. The external policy objectives of the Western
democracies are strictly limited. They are a promotion of national self-interest—a reaction to tactical moves by the Soviet
Union at that time—or else designed to enhance the profile of
an ambitious president or foreign minister, as was the case in
Germany. Naturally, we proclaim democracy, but this proclamation means about as much as the proclamation of Christianity by most Christians. Where democracy enters, as in Eastern
Europe, it doesn't enter because of our foreign policy but in spite

of it. It is the people who are fed up with totalitarian rulers. In general, Western foreign policy has prolonged the regimes of undemocratic governments. When the Soviets attacked Afghanistan, Jimmy Carter, then president of the United States, announced in a state of shock: "This aggression has changed my whole view of the Soviet Union." The obvious question is, What had his view been up to then? On what basis had foreign policy decisions been made?

In Western democracies, people want first and foremost to be left in peace to pursue their own activities. You mind your own business and I shall mind mine. If you leave me alone, I will not bother you—that is what we hear in every language from all corners of the democratic camp, sometimes wrapped up in the jargon of statesmen, sometimes expressed with total clarity. It is assumed that everyone else has the same objectives—personal and national self-interest. Such an assumption completely disregards the much more far-reaching objectives of the totalitarian and of some of the criminal rulers. We do not understand their objectives and how they go about achieving them.

The example of the 1936 Olympic Games in Berlin may help to clarify what I mean. Maybe some of the organizers had the same foggy idea George Bush had towards Saddam Hussein later on, namely to integrate Hitler into the family of nations. The same dumb opinion was uttered by Bill Clinton with regard to the North Korean leadership, whom he wants to make more cooperative by making concessions. The participating nations in Berlin in 1936 and their athletes saw the games as an international sports event in which they were eager to compete. Not so for the German government. For the Nazis it was a political occasion, a stepping stone to their more far-reaching objective of world conquest. For Hitler it was an international setting in which he could impress the Germans (especially the opposition), and he could demonstrate his power to the rest of the world. Gold medals came second and served principally to make the above points. Hitler was out to conquer the world for Germany—namely, his own rule. Western leaders had no concept of conquering Germany for democracy; they wanted to be left alone, so they appeased him. There never should have been

Olympic games in Berlin during the time of Nazi rule, and there should be none now in Beijing or Havana.

In Germany after 1945, the question asked all the time was, How could this have happened? One answer is that the aims of the Germans were too petty. The unemployed wanted work and Hitler promised them jobs. Thyssen and his industrialist friends believed that the Nazis could create and preserve employment and could also prevent the spread of communism among German workers with the concomitant ruin of German industry. They thought they could influence and control Hitler with their money. Hitler gave them full employment and took their money. The military leaders wanted to see the army freed from the bonds of the Versailles "peace treaty," so Hitler rebuilt the army. A majority of Germans also believed this treaty to be unjust and willingly endorsed Hitler's declared intention of obtaining its abrogation. Unlike Hitler, they did not see any further. The leaders of the conservative parties, Papen and Hugenberg, wanted to use Hitler for their own political ends and believed that they could control him. He ousted them when he didn't need them anymore. Millions of people showed total inertia and were neither on one side nor on the other; the immediate problems of their daily existence were their sole concern. Hitler's resolve and far-reaching objectives enabled him to promise everyone that their individual wishes would be met, so they supported him. Once his police state had been established, there was no going back. Goebbels once wrote in his diary: "When we gain power, we shall never abandon it again until our dead bodies are carried from our offices." And, that is exactly what happened.

The German industrialists of those days, such as Krupp, Thyssen, Reusch, Kirdorf, and others, were thinking first and foremost of the existence of their undertakings—the preservation of employment, of social stability, and of a Germany that would be strong enough to oppose the destructive economic dictates of the victorious powers of World War I—so as to regain at least some control over their own destiny. Their thinking and objectives followed traditional, national criteria that even in those days were no longer sufficient. They became Hitler's allies, partly in an endeavor to stem the spread of Communist influence in Germany. At the same time, Krupp, who was not a Nazi, had no qualms about establishing business relations with the Soviet Union when the possibility of exporting agricultural machinery arose. This particular transaction was negotiated at the government level. Krupp's decision to do business with the Soviet Union was no doubt greatly influenced by his bitterness at the senseless destruction of his factory installations by the Western allies under the dismantling provisions contained in the Treaty of Versailles. But, the decisive factor was the inability of that industrialist and nationally minded German to think in global power categories. Every development was viewed from the angle of its implications for his own situation, particularly profit.

Krupp's error was twofold: He failed to perceive the nature and aims of the Nazis, as well as those of the Soviets. He pursued his own limited objectives and thus paved the way for totalitarian systems. I do not know whether the apology "That is not what I wanted" was his, but it certainly does apply to countless thousands of Germans who thought like that when they realized what Hitler was doing.

The decisive superiority of Hitler, Stalin, and Gorbachev resides in the artistry with which they can delude mankind, while at the same time exploiting citizens and their institutions which have only limited aims to serve their own far-reaching objectives. The one hundred American businessmen who met in the autumn of 1995 in Colorado Springs with George Bush and Mikhail Gorbachev are as limited in their perspectives as were their German colleagues of that time. The only one in that group who had a plan as to where to take the world was Gorbachev.

The real aims of Western industrialists were made clear by Donald Kendall of the Pepsi-Cola company in a television interview in December 1988 about his company's engagement in the former Soviet Union: They are seeking profit—the reason for existence and objective of a capitalist undertaking. In reality, profit is simply the essential precondition for the financial health of a company in the context of more far-reaching economic and social objectives. But Kendall and others like him see profit as an end in itself. He therefore failed to understand Sen. Bill

Bradley, who told him in the same television interview that money invested or tied up in the Soviet Union might better be used in the developing countries, where the need is greater. Bradley obviously was referring to a value system which must be respected when funds are deployed, while Kendall recognized no particular values. This leads to brazen opportunism. Kendall believes that he is following a commercial policy. He may be very successful in the short term, but his lack of adequate objectives makes him easy to manipulate and exploit. The industrialists of the Nazi epoch did initially safeguard their full employment and economic growth, and the Communists ceased to play a political role in Germany. But the day of reckoning came in 1945: fifty-five million dead, Germany dishonored and destroyed, and the Soviet Union strongly entrenched in the heart of Europe.

Those who abetted the Nazi rise to power—and they were by no means all Germans—can be given the benefit of the doubt on one point: This was the first time that a godless, materialistic, and amoral ideology presented itself in the garb of a redeeming, democratic people's party, and it is therefore understandable that many people were deluded. This may be understandable, but it is not right and can never be so.

Looking at those who have abetted Soviet power for such a long time, I am not at all sure that the same understanding can be shown for their position. They have demonstrated that they have not learned the essential lesson of the Nazi disaster. As we saw earlier, an overwhelming majority of Germans today recognize that the Nazi leaders were criminals. Many consequences ensued from this. But the essential lesson was not learned, because hardly anyone understood the real nature of the events. And so the same appeasement was applied to the Soviet Union and China.

Individual and national objectives in the free world today are both inadequate. They are petty, selfish, and defensive. They contain the seed of self-destruction. On my travels in Germany and America over a period of many months, I questioned almost all the people I met about their aims in life. The unanimous answer was personal happiness and more money. My next question was, "What do you consider to be the aim of your congressman or senator?" My interlocutors all answered without hesitation, "To be re-elected."

According to a report in the *Los Angeles Times*, Ronald Reagan, referring to the Soviets in September 1985, said that living in the same world does not include the obligation to love one another or seek to change our respective systems. Henry Kissinger believed that we could not influence the internal development of the Soviet Union. That limitation lies at the root of the problem. The Russians, Poles, Letts, Ukrainians, Georgians—in short, all the enslaved people throughout the Soviet Empire—could have had their chains lifted many, many years earlier. Instead of helping the people who are demanding no more than their freedom, we have supported the slavemasters and weakened the position of the sufferers. The bill is now presented when we are being asked to pay up in order to prevent even greater disaster in the former Soviet Empire.

Similar disaster was sown in the developing countries. No objectives, except a vague idea of economic progress, existed. The countries of Latin America, Asia, and Africa were not treated according to their own merit, based on historical knowledge and appreciation, but were mainly used as pawns in the power struggle with the Soviets. In other words, we used them to a great extent for our own ends, and that is also true for the so-called development aid that I describe in another chapter. Since this treatment normally meant money for the ruling class, they were only too willing to be used in this way—a kind of prostitute mentality. It is the people who have to pay the price.

Besides the lack of purpose and the absence of overriding objectives of Western democracies, I consider our most serious deficiency to be moral decadence. As a matter of fact, moral decadence is a consequence of the former. Why should somebody who only thinks about himself and does not believe in God (or a life hereafter) have discipline in his daily life and forego the pleasures of fornication, eating, drinking, and the rest of it? To remake the government to renew America is without doubt a necessary task. But the objective is inadequate. It must also be said that promoting family values—as necessary as that is—is not good enough to beat the assault on moral values by the global Left and their grab for world power. There is only one objective adequate for every human being and every government leader, and that is to remake the world on the basis of God's absolute moral standards.

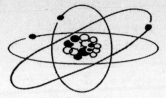

Lies

The Totalitarian Lie

The National Socialist Society in Germany was founded on the assumption of the superiority of the Aryan race. It consisted of a kind of superman, proclaiming the inferiority of the Jews, Slavs, and other people and races, combined with the historical task of the Nazi party to lead the German people towards their allotted destiny to dominate the world. The Nazi leaders were liars; their philosophy was a lie.

Communist society has been founded on the lie that history consists of a sequence of class conflicts based on injustice and inspired by hatred and that the Communist party is the organ charged with completing the last phase of historical development before the transition to a classless society. The party line laid down by the leaders is supposed to reflect historical truth, be generally binding, and be obeyed at all costs. Communist leaders are liars, too; their philosophy is a lie.

The lie inherent in both systems is the negation of the innate value of man, which is seen instead as deriving from the usefulness of the individual to society. The philosophy of the Nazis was a lie because there were no supermen among them or anywhere else. Most of the Nazis were men of low category who did not establish a people's community, but rather a police state in which they forced their own fiction onto everyone else in order to have a basis for the exercise of their power. Communists lie for precisely the same reason, only their fiction is different. In both cases, power is used to safeguard the position of the rulers. Since that position brings material benefits, it is reasonable to assert that lies are indulged in order to procure such benefits at the cost of others. To this is added the attractive proposition of "becoming like God," namely, of being able to wield unlimited power over other people who are told what they must think and do. If they fail to obey, they are excluded, or even liquidated. The laws and the whole judicial system become the instruments of a lie.

There is no classless society and never will be, just as there was no people's community of Nazi supermen. The two concepts arose in the brains of second rate "philosophers" and were passed off on the Germans and Russians as a historic revelation which was then imposed by force. Fortunately enough, the Nazi horror lasted for only twelve years, albeit with a terrible toll in blood. The Communist lie has, however, already been in power for more than seventy-five years and is eating like a cancer at the body of man. The "disinformation" department of the KGB has been a source of an unending stream of lies based on master-liar Joseph Goebbels' thesis that if you repeat a lie long enough, something will always stick. Lies sow hatred and dissent. It will take generations before the consequences of this unscrupulous and subversive activity can be overcome. And there is no evidence that it has stopped. The task has even been taken over by Western media.

Some years ago, the German professor Martin Kriele made the following report on the Sandinists Ernesto Cardenal and Miguel d'Escoto when they were still in power in Nicaragua. On the occasion of their official visit to Germany, they laughed at the stupidity of the Germans. "These Germans believe every word. They believe everything we tell them about our democratic intentions. We are Communists, but they just do not want to accept the fact. So be it. If that is the condition for them to give us money, we shall milk the stupid cow."[1] For a Communist, a lie is not a lie but a tactical weapon in the struggle for power. It was Lenin who had made lying part of Communist philosophy, explaining that a lie is justified by the ends. Theft comes next, as I explain later.

Gorbachev was furious when Helmut Kohl compared him with Goebbels. He probably felt himself slighted, as though Albert Einstein was compared with a physics teacher in a secondary school. Since he has (to my knowledge) never disavowed Marxism or Leninism, he has remained, over all the years, the leading representative of a philosophy of lies and violence that is independent of economic reform. I therefore consider it likely that he has been so enmeshed in his own tissue of lies that he can no longer distinguish between truth and falsehood—that he equates his own lies with truth.

The West has never understood the nature of the totalitarian systems. It has reacted against the symptoms and acted on the political, military, and economic front, while the ideological level—the battle between truth and lie—has never been addressed. It is on that level only that a permanent victory of free society over totalitarian society can be achieved. The reason for ignoring the decisive ideological struggle is very simple: we are on the wrong side of the battle line; we are liars ourselves, and we do not recognize the lies which form an integral part of our democratic structures. What holds us still and prevents our ultimate defeat is first the fact that our forefathers injected truth into the structures of our societies, which are not that easy to eliminate (as hard as some try); and second, that millions of people stick to their faith in God and to basic ethics. But, they are on the defensive and in a losing battle since they lack the commitment to absolute truth as a global issue and the understanding of the raging power struggle to which every local and national issue has to be related.

Vaclav Havel, now president of the Czech Republic and a dissident at the time of Communist rule in his country, defined the role of lies in the following way:

> Life is entangled in a web of hypocrisy and lie: the power of the bureaucracy is called the power of the people; the working class is being enslaved in the name of the working class; the total humiliation of man is defined as ultimate liberation of man, shutting off information is proclaimed to be free information; the manipulation through power calls itself public control of power, abuse is named

adherence to legal order, suppression of culture is presented as its development; extension of imperial influence is said to be help to the oppressed, lack of freedom of expression is praised as highest form of liberty and the joke of a superficial election process becomes the highest form of democracy; the prohibition of independent thinking is scientific philosophy and occupation becomes brotherly help. State power must falsify because it is a prisoner of its own lies; it falsifies past, present and future and falsifies statistical facts; it pretends not to have an all-powerful police state but says it is respecting human rights; it pretends not to persecute anybody; it pretends not to be afraid; it pretends not to pretend anything.[2]

"People do not need to believe all these mystifications, but everybody must behave in such a way as whether he believes it, must tolerate it in silence or at least put himself on a good footing with those who operate these mystifications. That means he must live in the lie. He does not need to accept the lie. It is enough that he accepts life with the lie. Therewith it is confirmed that he fills the system, he makes it—he is the system."[3]

Under the surface of the "life in the lie," describes Havel, are the real aspirations and beliefs of people, a hidden openness to truth which can explode any time and therefore constitutes a constant danger for totalitarian power, because it is not controllable. The confrontation of this opposition with power is not on the level of institutions with organized instruments of power, but is on the level of the existence of the individual. This power cannot be measured in quantities—there are no battalions of soldiers nor organizations to get hold of. It is rather a kind of underground fifth column which spreads with great speed to all those who are gripped by truth, says Havel. To live a "life in truth," he explains, is a moral act, which everybody can perform. To this add that truth is the only answer to a lie. When truth becomes the weapon of free society, the need for atomic missiles will disappear.

Alexander Solzhenitsyn pointed out precisely the same in 1974:

Our present system is unique in world history, because over and above its physical and economic constraints, it demands of us total surrender of our souls, continuous and active participation in the general, conscious lie. To this putrefaction of the soul, this spiritual enslavement, human beings, who wish to be human cannot consent. When Caesar having exacted what is Caesar's, demands still more insistently that we render unto him what is God's—that is a sacrifice we dare not make.

The most important part of our freedom, inner freedom, is always subject to our will. If we surrender it to corruption, we do not deserve to be called human.

But let us note that if the absolutely essential task is not political liberation, but the liberation of our souls from participation in the lie forced upon us, then it requires no physical, revolutionary, social, organizational measures, no meetings, strikes, trade unions. No. It requires from each individual a moral step within his or her power—no more than that. No one who voluntarily runs with the hounds of falsehood, will ever be able to justify himself to the living, or to posterity, or to his friends, or to his children.[4]

"DO NOT LIE!" he calls out to his compatriots. "DO NOT TAKE PART IN THE LIE! DO NOT SUPPORT THE LIE!"[5]

Lenin, and also Hitler, knew that individuals who obey a higher moral code and those who consider God more important than their self-appointed human overlords, cannot be manipulated indefinitely with lies, and will one day come into conflict with the philosophy which despises human beings. The American Civil Liberties Union seems to have the same fear when they, in a letter to me and others, referred to the "hateful speeches of Pat Robertson" and his "pro-family Christians" organized in the dangerous Christian Action bent on imposing Christian morality on the rest of the nation. They called for help to stop them. I wish there were more Pat Robertsons around because he does not force anything upon anybody, but exposes the lies with great courage and insight.

"We wish to be true believers and at the same time recognize the Soviet Union as our earthly home. Its joys and successes are our successes. Any blow directed at the Soviet Union will be experienced as a blow against us." That was the vow of obedience which the bishops of the Russian Orthodox Church had to pledge to Stalin. The basic contradiction in this is that nobody can serve the lie and the truth at the same time. A compromise with truth means the automatic alliance with the lie, as we learned in Nazi Germany. In the Soviet Union, the churches were defined as houses of prayer and the activity of the church was confined by law to prayer in those houses. It was forbidden to propagate religious teachings in public, and no interference in society and state affairs was permitted, as in Nazi Germany. The church as an organization was turned into an instrument of Soviet policy with the primary aim of deluding naive (or should I say dumb?) Western churchmen and politicians. The top hierarchy positions, including that of the patriarch, were filled with KGB agents. Atheist Gorbachev must be very happy, as atheist Hitler would be, that after their own demise, the ACLU and their likes are actively engaged in making Nazi and Communist practices the law in the United States of America.

The Concept and Power of the Lie

The American psychotherapist Dr. Scott Peck describes "people of the lie" as all those who have handed themselves over to evil. The phenomenon, namely, the possession of an individual by lies, is not confined to Nazis and Communists. The fundamental error of the "anti's," to whomever they may be opposed, lies in the assumption that the bad men are always on the other side, while they themselves belong to the good.

It is not that a Communist is evil per se while a democrat is good. The evil is in everyone, including in each one of us. The principal question is, To what extent does evil determine our action—is a person or a nation guided by selfish aims which we cover with lies, or by ethical standards which exclude the lie?

What is different between "them" and "us" is simply the basis of society at any time, the degree of the penetration of lies into the system, and the objectives which prevail. I could agree readily with Ronald Reagan when he spoke of the "evil empire," because a totalitarian state—Nazi, Communist, or any other form—is nothing but the organized form of a lie, on which all government structures are built. Reagan hit the nail on the head, but there was a mistake in his reaction to evil and his concept of good. As a result, he stepped back from his assertion because he believed that it might be harmful to developing better relations. Like most Westerners, he wavered between anti-communism and appeasement. Both attitudes are barren and, in the end, merely promote the things which we claim to be fighting and then later adapt.

The Lie in Our Society

We therefore must now consider the role assumed by lies in our free society. The German philosopher Karl Jaspers defines lies as follows:

> One may lie by language by deliberately asserting something which is false. It means lying to others but not to oneself, one is misusing language. But a further step is also possible. By lying, the lie may reach a state in which a person finally believes his own lies so that the distinction between truth and falsehood is lost. . . . Untruth may range from the shameless lie which is immediately recognizable as such to a total, inextricable system of lies which is put forward with the conviction of an actor who no longer perceives himself as an actor. The individual is then trapped in his own world of lies. Words have lost their consistent sense. Sometimes they are understood in the same way as the interlocutor understands them and then they are taken to mean the opposite.[6]

Thus lies are elevated into a principle. As Jaspers puts it, "Truth and fiction are combined in such a way that nothing good arises, but the radical lie itself becomes reality."[7]

The free Western world is becoming increasingly remote from the truths on which it was originally based and is turning to lies. These lies have many names. Joseph Goebbels, Hitler's chief of liars, was a master of packaging lies, to make dirt appear beautiful and so incite the Germans to follow a suicide path. He would be very pleased to look at our society of today. Our lies, like his, appear in the shimmering light of beauty, pretending to represent the best of contemporary thinking, creating the illusion of progress and salvation, the sensation that finally after such a long time of failure, we are now achieving what is good for people.

We call freedom of choice what in reality is the right to kill. The refined ability to manipulate voters for profit becomes the democratic process, we say lifestyle to perversion and claim self-ishness to be national interest. Does the American Constitution legislate the division of government and God? It is a lie, for it does not. All consequent legislation and Supreme Court rulings on this issue are based on a lie. Is a homosexual born to be a homosexual and in need of protection? It is a lie since he *can* change, as anyone else can change. All subsequent legislation and court rulings are again based on a lie. Are women to be the same as men? No, it too is a lie. The promoters of all of these concepts are servants of the lie.

There is the suggestion that each individual is entitled to enjoy his life according to his own criteria and to devote his existence to his own pleasure. Something which was only one aspect of the Declaration of Independence of the American founding fathers has for many people become an absolute. St. Augustine called living for oneself a lie because it contradicts the truth which God has implanted in us: to serve Him, to whom we owe obedience. The consequence of the rejection of this truth—and of obedience to it—must not be acknowledged pri-marily in the personal religious sphere, into which we have con-fined God but where truth is no longer taken seriously. The acceptance of the multiple forms of lies as equally legitimate social forces constitutes a fundamental error of our contempo-rary epoch from which most of our social problems originate. The personal sector is merely the starting platform. The power of lies in our free society and its democratic structures springs from the lies enacted by millions of men and women in their lives.

When I watched the press conference of Anita Hill in which she described for the first time in public the sexual harassment she had supposedly suffered, I was shocked because I thought, nobody can invent a story like this and make it public in such a convincing way; it must therefore be true. Later on I came to the conclusion that she was lying. The point to be made is that the issue was not sexual harassment, but truth vs. lie. The fact that it was seemingly so difficult to determine the truth in something which became a national and international issue, shows how far we have gone and how far we have been taken over by lies.

There is another aspect to the story which I did not hear anybody raise. According to Hill, she followed Clarence Thomas to the Agency for Equal Opportunity from the Ministry of Education because she could not afford to lose her job. At the same time, she wanted to work for the less privileged, a field of work she said she liked. Two lies are exposed here that are independent of the principal one.

1. If it would have been true that the principal law enforcement officer in the agency was violating the very spirit and rules he swore to enact, then she, by not speaking up immediately and attempting to correct that unacceptable situation, would have greatly contributed to making the government's efforts to help the underprivileged void since the truthfulness and effectiveness of any institution depend on the integrity of the people at the top. Therefore, she could not have been really interested in the welfare of those she said she was trying to help.

2. According to her own statement, her fear of losing her job had priority over her fighting for justice. As I mention later in this book, it was precisely the fear of not just losing one's job but one's life which made millions of Germans silent and cooperative when they should have stood up to Hitler. It is the appeasers of wrong who bring disaster to their nations.

In 1938 Hitler got rid of General von Fritsch, the conservative commander in chief of the German army. Von Fritsch was accused of being a homosexual. It was a lie which was fabricated on purpose to pave the way for Hitler to become the commander in chief. Fritsch resigned and Hitler took over. A little later Hitler managed to oust Fieldmarshal von Blomberg, commander in chief of the armed forces, and combined therewith the two commands in his hands. Since at that time Hitler was riding high in public opinion with unheard-of political and economic successes, provided to an extent by the appeasing Western governments, the other generals resented what was done, especially to von Fritsch, but did not stand up to Hitler and did

nothing about it. This cowardliness had to be paid for dearly by
the German nation because it was the beginning of the military
disaster Hitler led us into. This story makes it clear, in my view,
that political and economic achievements of the day are no real
indication of where a nation is heading. The moral indicators
are the decisive ones.

An existential lie develops out of a series of lies, first towards oneself and then towards others, until in the end lying
becomes a habit. I know people who are deeply convinced that
they are benefactors to others and to society, while in reality they
are ruthless crooks. There is no difference between a Nazi or
Communist liar and a liar in a democracy. I repeat, the difference rests in the extent to which the structure of society—the
constitution, the legal system, the political procedures, practices
of life, and business—is based on lie or truth. There is, of course,
also the difference in objectives and the means one is prepared
to use. In a totalitarian system, all power is given to the rulers,
but not to the ruled, which is proof of the rottenness of the
philosophy. In our free society, we are trying very hard to get to
the same principle. Only slightly changed personal objectives
justify the means; ethical restrictions become more and more
obsolete, and each one believes he has a democratic right to his
selfishness and pursuit of anything which is advantageous and
enjoyable to himself. That concept is based on a lie. It is also a
lie that governments have the right to pursue national selfishness (which is normally defined as national interest) at the expense of others. While government structures in our society are
still widely different from totalitarian government structures,
moral differences are disappearing. That can only lead to similar
legal structures with the consequence of arbitrary use of political
power. That is the new world order which is presently surfacing.

One day at noon, one of my long-time business partners sat
down exhausted at my desk, figuratively wiping the sweat from
his brow. He groaned that he had spent four hours in the factory
repairing the welding machine. I was impressed. The fact is,
however, he had spent no more than five minutes in the factory
and had not touched the welding machine, which was working
normally. Similar scenes were repeated frequently. Very much
later, the most accurate explanation of this theater of lies ap-

peared to me to reside in the fact that he did not simply want to impress me, but to also fill me with fear that I could not run the factory without him.

Krupp Steel, a steelworks company, once delivered to our plant in Mexico City almost forty tons of poor quality steel. They admitted on our reclamation that there had been a fault in the production process. We ran the risk of damaging our machines by using this steel, but had no other choice but to use the steel if we did not want to close down the factory and lose our purchase orders. The damage, apart from the risk to the machines, resulted in a wastage rate of the raw material which was too high for us to absorb. It then transpired that the specifications which Krupp had received from us were inaccurate. My partner had travelled to Germany every year at the company's expense, but had never looked into this matter and never visited the steel manufacturer. He now visited Krupp to complain, claiming that all of their steel was unusable. He asked for payment for the entire forty tons plus all additional expenses like transport, custom duties, etc. When I arrived at the steelworks six weeks later (in a state of alarm because of our cheating), I found that preparations were being made to either have the steel specially reprocessed in Mexico or to take it all back again. We were close to being caught as liars and could not have received a penny by way of compensation; I decided to tell them the truth about the situation, and we easily agreed on the amount of compensation.

The lie by my partner belonged to the category of primitive lying. He wanted to achieve an immediate material benefit and knew he was lying. Many people use lies of this kind without thinking very much about it or considering whether the lie damages anyone else. It has become nearly a normal procedure to gain an advantage for oneself or one's company by making something appear better than it is, misstating the facts. Perhaps the old adage that lies are easily caught is not often as immediately applicable as in our steel case. What is quite certain is that this is an example of the extent to which lies have taken root in our democracies. What astonished me later on was the fact that my partner was able to feed a constant stream of lies to me with the most innocent expression in the world. He simply opened his mouth and lied. I was then able to observe in our business community the same behavior in others who boldly distorted truth to gain small personal benefits with the result that they, too, became caught up in their own web of lies and were convinced they were decent people when they were the contrary of it.

"We no longer know how to survive with truth in the economic daily struggle," said a supplier of the Volkswagen Mexico plant to me. "We got accustomed to a society of lies." He referred to the inflated and dishonest cost calculations, which most of the suppliers, with the exception of me, consistently presented to the plant. Various automotive companies, I believe, have established this procedure for anyone who wants to sell something to them, so that the plant is able to influence the price in its favor—understandable, since they need to be competitive in the price of the final product, the car. I have successfully rejected this procedure, received a number of insults from the lower level, had to withstand pressure, and lived through some very difficult weeks, very afraid to lose my base business. I neither wanted to make lies the basis of a business relationship nor did I want to accept outside interference in my own price determination and profit margins. In the long run, I found my position was respected and personal relationships were not only undamaged but fortified.

One thus detects the same character trait exposed in the Nazis and Communists also in us. Since the liars I referred to are certainly not Communists, their action can perhaps best be described as a kind of moral Bolshevism, as a friend of mine, Frank Buchman, has called it. The Soviet system—like that of the Nazis in Germany—is nothing other than a highly organized form of lies. It does not present itself simply as an occasional untruth spoken out loud, but as the institutionalized expression of character decomposition and rot which is reflected everywhere in the rules of society, in legislation, in the repression of minorities, and in action taken toward the rest of the world. It includes the effort organized at state levels to impose the lie on others and ultimately on the whole world.

This character rot has grown up out of our Western society. Greed, indifference, carelessness, cupidity, exploitation, and the lies of some have generated envy and hatred in others; a desire for revenge has led to an organized form of characterlessness, justified by the theories and doctrines of philosophers who were equally lacking in character: communism and nazism and their respective states. The factors which caused them to emerge in the first place continue spreading throughout the free world in each one of us.

Vaclav Havel expressed this truth many years ago:

> Referring to the relationship between Western Europe and the totalitarian states, I believe the biggest mistake Europe could make is the one it is most exposed to: not to conceive the totalitarian systems as what they are in the final analysis, namely the convex mirror of the whole modern civilisation and a strong—and perhaps the last— call to this civilisation for a complete revision of its understanding of self. . . . I cannot but believe that western civilisation is threatened much more by itself than by SS-20 missiles.[8]

U.S. News and World Report headlined its 23 February 1988 edition "A Nation of Liars?" and described the alarming breakdown of basic honesty in America. The article referred, for example, to the estimate by a congressional subcommittee that roughly one in three Americans in gainful employment had falsified the documents on the basis of which they were recruited. "There is a growing degree of cynicism and sophistication in our society," says the former White House press secretary, Jody Powell, "a sense that all things are relative, and nothing is absolutely right or wrong." Robert Nisbet of Columbia University adds, "The number of certain misdemeanors in the universities has risen—falsifications and inaccurate research claims are on the increase. Perhaps I am naive, but fifty years ago there was a code of honor among investment specialists and brokers which one can hardly find today. The whole fabric of society is breaking apart and more and more lies are being told." "To the extent family life is disintegrating, kids are not being taught values about lying, cheating and stealing," explained the president of Notre Dame University, Theodore Hesburgh. The *U.S. News and World Report* article concludes with an observation by

Gary Edwards, executive director of the Ethics Resource Center in Washington: "A free and open society requires a high degree of ethical conduct, since people must have confidence in their institutions and leaders. . . . If confidence in the country's government breaks down, apathy, cynicism and in the last resort anarchy will result." It remains only to be added that once a society reaches this stage, totalitarian rulers have an easy time of it. In a 1991 Gallup poll during the Thomas Hearings, the lack of confidence in government institutions by the American people clearly showed up; only the presidency and the armed forces did relatively well. No more than 18 percent expressed confidence in Congress, the lowest rating ever. Newspapers, which like other non-government institutions were included in the poll, received an approval rate of only 32 percent. Seventy-five percent of Americans in 1995 considered their own government to be untrustworthy.

The journalist Lars Eric Nelson writes under a Washington byline: "Of course a number of lies must be expected of every government. It is impossible to conduct diplomacy or guarantee national security without deception. A President who claims 'I shall never lie to you' as Jimmy Carter did, will go down in history as a fool who is incapable of taking part in the game of the great powers."[9] He goes on to list eighteen lies which were proved as such by comparing the statements of the various participants at the start of the Iran arms affair. A great many lies were added later on and if, applying Nelson's theory, the number of lies is extrapolated to the number of governments in the world, we arrive at astronomic figures for the numbers of lies pronounced at the government level each year.

It is no wonder that problems can no longer be solved but instead are passed on from one liar to another. At the same time, the skill is developed of presenting things, especially in the political sphere, in such a way that other persons or groups are always purported to be guilty of the prevailing miserable state of affairs. To the honor of American democracy, the basic concept that a lie is unacceptable still exists. Regrettably, however, all that is really done is to attempt to disclose the lies of others, while pretending that oneself would not act in the same way.

The loss of substance and the loss of any long-term perspective is thus advancing.

As I explained, the Nazi and Communist systems were nothing but the organized form of a lie. I now begin to suspect that our democratic governments come very close to the same definition. Contrary to authoritarian rule, democratic rule is supposed to come from the people and be exercised by the people for the people. In reality, even though there is an element "from the people," which is stronger in some countries than in others, it appears that the class called "the establishment," to which some elected people also belong, rules—not for the people but for themselves and against all others. The establishment rules by lying. Facts are being distorted, opponents are being smeared, statistics are being manipulated, and the people are first induced and then forced to pay taxes which amount to a multiple of what is needed to maintain the ruling class. The difference between the two systems is that here the expropriation is done via taxes— we give to them—while there the rulers took the whole cake at the outset and then gave a little to the people, keeping the main bulk for themselves.

When leaders fail to exercise restraint in their personal lives, they also fail to lead their countries as they should. Among the heads of state in Latin America and the Caribbean, a large number unfortunately follow the adulterous practices of Western leaders like John F. Kennedy. Here, too, one can only shudder at the political consequences, since the rule that a man cannot live crooked and think straight applies equally in all cases. We have come to accept the idea that we may get into any bed and couple like dogs if we feel like it. It is a lie. Those who cannot control their appetites are unfit for government.

I was left almost speechless when I watched a discussion between a group of experts, among them a Cabinet member, on German television on the subject of AIDS. Not one of them mentioned the possibility that Western sexual philosophy and practices might be at fault.

Just as people tend to skirt most problems without having the courage to recognize the core of the problem, so the AIDS epidemic is not dealt with at its roots. Instead, efforts are made to limit the risk with explanations about the danger, condoms, tests, and controls. In fact, the problem is very simple, as the former German Health Minister Rita Sussmuth points out in her book entitled *AIDS*, quoting from Friedrich Deinhart: "AIDS is admittedly the most dangerous illness of all, but it is also the easiest to avoid." Put bluntly, this means that the right to sleep around must be adjured as a lie. I heard the head of the American agency to fight AIDS state that he planned to order a study on the sexual behavior of young people to determine what motivates them. Seldom have I heard something so ridiculous. He does not need an expensive study, because the answer to the question is obvious: lust. That has to be dealt with by parents, teachers, and the media. And it is just as easy with all the other problems mentioned. It should not be hard for those involved to identify their particular lies. For the politicians who normally act on the principle of preferring votes to truth, the act of self-renunciation may be even harder than for the rest of us, but it is the only way to a solution.

The modern warfare is not between armies and fleets of different nations, even though it could take that form. The cultural ideological war for the control of humanity is the battle between truth and lie in the heart of every human being. There is no neutrality, and you are either on the one side or on the other. The enemy does not necessarily have the passport of another country; he might be sitting in your own government reciting patriotic themes and collecting taxes. He who is a liar is the enemy of his country and his people.

Do Americans, remembering Nazi Germany or the Soviet Union, really believe that it cannot happen here? I tell you, it is happening. America is in the pre-totalitarian stage. The murky bowl of lies covering our world must be destroyed with the hammer of truth.

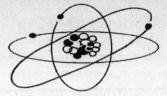

Money

Late one evening as I walked out onto the street from my lawyer's office in Mexico City, the headlights of a car were switched on, straight at me. They were turned off again immediately and the night became as dark as before. But the lights had been on long enough for the occupants of the car to recognize me. A black Renault was parked on the center strip of the divided highway.

My heart beat faster. I was not sure whether I was facing a real threat or whether my imagination was playing tricks on me. Were the two men in the car looking for me, or just waiting for a friend whom they did not want to miss? I quickly crossed the street and began to walk against the oncoming traffic. If somebody followed me in a car, he could now only reach me from in front and not surprise me from the rear. I walked as fast as I could to my house, looking back regularly over my shoulder to make sure no one was following me. Nothing happened, and I was back home in ten minutes.

In Mexico everything is possible. The rule of law is largely theoretical. A uniform is often the only distinguishing feature between policemen and gangsters. Somebody I knew had to flee the country with his family, not because he was guilty of any misdemeanor, but because somebody wanted to get rid of him for business reasons and had paid a great deal of money to have charges fabricated by a lawyer's office. On the advice of connoisseurs in this matter, my friend had taken his family with him to prevent them from being used as hostages in his absence to blackmail him. In Mexico, the obligation is on the defendant to prove his own innocence, and the principle that the accused is innocent until he is proven guilty does not apply. This lays the door wide open to arbitrary acts. A defendant may rot in prison without trial. And a trial is no guarantee of justice either. Two traffic policemen were recently arrested by the criminal police during an armed attack on a supermarket. They were interned in the central police station. The streets around the building were almost immediately cordoned off by patrol vehicles. Policemen occupied the surrounding roofs, and after a brief exchange of shots, the two uniformed robbers were released.

That evening, outside my attorney's office, I was not only trying to escape from the police; I was also afraid of drastic measures by a business associate whom I had once considered a close friend but who later revealed his true face as an unscrupulous trickster. He once said to me, "I make use of everyone I meet to enrich myself." Unfortunately I did not establish any connection between his philosophy of life and myself, so I did not take him seriously. Also, I failed to reflect on the character of a man who expresses such views. I now know that for the sake of money, he would not stop at destroying the lives and existence of others, even of persons close to him. He would sell his grandmother if the price was right, as we say in Germany.

In 1981, I had invited him to take over a division of our automobile components manufacturing plant, in which I made him represent my shares and those of our German partners. My "honorable and efficient" friend, who received part of the capital, accepted all that he obtained from me and began his attempt to box me in so as to gain control of the plant. He wanted to get all. I did not realize what he was doing and practically handed myself over to him by giving him far-reaching powers-of-attorney and appointing his brother-in-law head of our administration, although our little firm did not need such an official. I had in mind our future projects, which we were supposed to share equally between us. Those projects were to legitimize his participation in my company, but he brought nothing in return. Instead, he got rid of my production manager and my secretary. The time came when I began to recognize the facts.

I felt myself exposed to growing pressures, especially when I learned that he was telling other people that I was actually good for nothing and that, in the long run, he would have to exclude me from the business since his own money was at stake.

The horrible thing about it was that I had myself given him the possibility of carrying out his threats since I lacked at that time the necessary immigration status in Mexico which allowed me to invest. In my blind trust, I had put all that was mine in his name. I was at the mercy of a ruthless profiteer. I avoided all conflicts and gave in, even when it hurt, until I managed to restore the original situation of the company, in which I represented the majority. I then initiated a complicated and cumbersome legal procedure to withdraw his powers-of-attorney.

It was during those weeks in which I had endless discussions with various lawyers that the street incident occurred which I described earlier. That very day he had set the police on me under a formal pretext, and I had been obliged to take refuge in my lawyer's office with my razor, dollars, and passport. It was on the same evening that the headlights of the parked car troubled me so much. A general assembly of shareholders had been convened for the next day and was due to make a decision on the powers-of-attorney. If I disappeared, he would keep control of the company with his powers. As I was dealing with a greedy and unscrupulous trickster, I could not rule out violence. I therefore hired a bodyguard for the day of the shareholders' meeting, and my unscrupulous associate lost his power-of-attorney.

During all that time I was fighting a bitter struggle for my own existence. The production of our factory had fallen to one-third of its normal level because of the shortage of spare parts, poor quality raw materials, and completely inadequate machine maintenance. Our cash flow was insufficient, and I had to run up substantial personal debts in order to maintain production and at least minimal sales, while trying to remedy the deficiencies. A number of export orders were lost and for several months we were verging on the abyss of bankruptcy.

As I later learned, my colleague (who, unlike me, had a sound financial base) had quite deliberately brought our engineering service and the firm as a whole into this situation to starve me out financially and then get rid of me cheaply. He had informed our German partners that the rectifier on our welding machine needed to be replaced and that the factory would have to be closed for three months for a general overhaul, the cost of which he estimated at four hundred thousand dollars. He then offered to buy their share in the business. He obviously thought that we were stupid enough to take all this at face value. The rectifier had already been replaced one year previously at a cost of some thirty-three hundred dollars, as I quickly informed our German partners by telephone. The firm had only been closed on Sundays and public holidays, and neither before nor after this time were we forced to shut down for a longer period of time because of repairs. Because of technical problems, which he had produced deliberately, the company was now nearly paralyzed for about ten months.

How relieved I was when early in 1987 production reached full capacity again. A great many things then came to light, including outright thefts. The man I had entrusted my plant to had repeatedly removed our pushrod tubes from the factory using a noncompany car and driver; he then sold this material for his personal profit without informing me. On each occasion he sent his business card with an order to our supervisors. The next day he asked for the card back and destroyed it. The supervisors had been instructed by him to say nothing to me about this and other occurrences. They did not particularly like what was happening, but they did not dare contradict their immediate superior. Very much later, when my supervisors were quite sure that my dishonest colleague had no more say-so in the firm, I received a full report on the facts.

Without my knowledge, he also laid a pipeline from our factory to another one next door in which he held a majority of the shares and where he manufactured medical instruments. He used our compressors to pump air into his own plant. At the end, I got rid of him as a partner in the manufacturing company, but he managed to keep stolen land and the building.

Dishonest partners are no longer unusual. A doctor friend of mine in the southern United States ran a joint practice with a friend. The agreement was that all their income should be pooled and shared between them once their overheads had been covered. To his horror, my friend found out one day that his partner was making arrangements with patients under the table and diverting the proceeds to his own account. This reached such a scale that the very livelihood of my friend was at risk, a fact which did not bother his greedy partner.

Money is a vital part of our lives. We need it to pay for our subsistence, the education of our children, travel to other countries—in short we cannot do without money. I do not have the slightest objection to possessing as much money as possible. Untold problems which one has to face every day are attributable to the lack of sufficient funds. However, the fundamental question is, What priority should money take in the life of each individual? Some people would walk over others' dead bodies to get more. The desire for more money sometimes displaces all other considerations and becomes the main purpose in life. Acquiring money becomes an end in itself and dominates an individual's thoughts and actions. Value standards are distorted and human relations sacrificed; the family is placed in second or even in a lower place. Many family ties even break completely. Among businessmen in particular, there are those who have fallen prey to the attraction of money and give the desire for more first place in their lives. Unfortunately, I have had to deal with several of them. They are not to be envied, even if they do manage to amass vast quantities of ready cash with which they can avoid all material worries.

Since the acquisition of money cannot be an adequate goal for life in itself, it makes no one happy. The individual who hungers after money can never get enough. He will hardly ever have any real friends. He passes over the real values in life because he does not understand them. In short, when money becomes an idol, it destroys the character and soul of the person who worships that idol. I have met poor people who lead a much happier life than quite a lot of rich people.

Hardly anyone would openly describe himself as greedy. Some call their greed a healthy "desire for success," which "surely cannot be wrong." To say that one "represents business interests" also sounds fine, but the phrase may just cover a reckless pursuit of selfishness. Each person needs to look honestly into his own heart to define the reality of his motivation. How, then, do things seem?

Thinking and acting based on commercial criteria has become normal and is destroying the very foundations of our civilization. More and more people link their decisions exclusively to the advantages they think they can achieve. They pass this spirit of selfishness on to the next generation.

At no point has the necessity of fighting for our existence had priority over our family life. My wife and I have lived through quite a number of financial catastrophes in our twenty-three years of marriage. When I got married, well-meaning friends advised me to make a contract so that I would not get hurt economically in case the marriage should break up. Obviously, the preoccupation with possible financial disadvantages outweighs the will to commit oneself to the person with whom one wants to build a common life, and that demands sacrifice of self. Perhaps we refugees who lost all our possessions overnight have a deeper insight into what is essential in life. Since 1945, I see my possessions as something temporary, even though there are special values attached to some belongings because they were very hard to acquire. Nobody can guarantee that I will not suffer economic or financial disaster one day. In any case, when I die I can take nothing with me.

Corporative methods leave more and more to be desired. Ethics are often deemed old-fashioned, and the maximization of profits has become the slogan of managers. The search for short-term profits, which can then be highlighted in the quarterly report, is depriving stock exchanges of their true function of procuring capital on the one hand, and providing solid investment opportunities on the other. It is turning them instead into a casino to satisfy the cupidity of the players.

Financial swindlers like Ivan Boesky and others of his ilk are regrettably not isolated phenomena but only the extreme manifestation of the ordinary American's hunger for money: "Greed has become socially acceptable in Wall Street and in America," writes Ken Auletta in his book *Greed and Glory in Wall Street.*[1] The corporate policy of Lehman Brothers, one of the oldest finance houses in New York, centered, according to Auletta, on the ambition and cupidity of the partners whose primary interest lay in the acquisition of personal wealth. This aim, which set one partner against the other and began to replace the tradition of providing a genuine service, broke the company apart; it was eventually taken over and incorporated into Shearson/American Express.

For this and other reasons (which I shall be looking at later), the enterprise United States of America (and with it the free world) is also in the process of breaking apart. The partners at Lehman were primarily concerned with their own bonuses. As long as the bonuses were high, they persistently overlooked other "less essential" factors. The personal income of almost every one of them exceeded the total annual sales of my factory in its best days, which shows that prosperity is a relative concept and it appears difficult to define an absolute degree of satisfaction.

The number of people in all income groups who simply cannot get enough money, regardless of how much they already have, is on the increase. This phenomenon goes hand-in-hand with the destruction of families and the undermining of democratic institutions. For most people, the important factor is not an absolute amount which they would consider sufficient, but a comparison with what others earn. Cupidity generates envy and hatred, explosive factors in any society.

At least some of the Lehman partners felt that their professional conduct, which was aimed primarily at amassing more and more money by any means whatsoever, was in conflict with their duties as citizens and with their ethical code. However, the next generation may no longer feel these pangs of conscience. We are on a slippery downward slope. The principle that the aim of profit maximization justifies the means (Marxist philosophy in a different package) is beginning to win the day, although individuals fail to notice because everyone around them subscribes to the same principle. The individual belongs to the pack or the crowd, as Auletta puts it.

The description of the Lehman story is particularly enlightening; it "reminds us that human relations mean at least as much if not more than figures on the balance sheet," comments Auletta. Peterson, former secretary of commerce under Richard Nixon (who did not have the faintest idea of what was going on with the people around him), pursued his own projects and the acquisition of money in a decent manner. Glucksmann, the "bad guy," eased his partner out of the top position and then completely out of the company because he believed that he could find real "fulfillment only by assuming the sole direction of the firm."[2] If his urge for the power accruing from the chairmanship of the board was fed by a spirit of bitterness at not being recognized, his actions were inspired by the same driving force which motivated Hitler and Lenin, only within another framework. I am talking about motives, not actions, of course. Some partners compared the company messengers with the Nazi SA. Purges were compared with those of Stalin, and when Glucksmann, the Eastern European descendant of Hungarian Jews, failed to gain admission to the renowned Century Club in Westchester because he did not belong to the accepted descendants of the German Jews, he shouted at William Bernback, who notified him of the refusal: "You are one of those Jews who should be sent to the gas chambers."[3]

In his book, Auletta describes the human raw material that has made the totalitarian power structures of the Nazis and Soviets possible: Hatred, envy, cupidity and lust for power, lies, fear, unscrupulousness, and selfishness. The dividing lines did not run between black and white men, Aryans and Jews, rich and poor, but between bankers and dealers, the "ins" and "outs," the Eastern and Western Jews. For some people, money is a way of acquiring and exercising power. For others, power is a way of obtaining all that money can procure. If the objectives of Western man are defined in terms of money and those of the Soviets (or Nazis) in terms of power, it is easy to recognize that both are the expression of the same materialism. The greedy capitalist and the power-hungry Communist have fallen prey to the same evil spirit.

The attempt to enrich oneself at the cost of others is nothing new. Dishonesty has existed as long as man himself. The new aspect is that it has now come to be accepted as a normal pattern of conduct and has even been consecrated on a philosophical basis. When I was a student in Hamburg and engaged in a debate with the chairman of the Communist students' union in the university, I told him how I had conducted a lively trade in stolen tomatoes and cucumbers when I was a worker in a large horticultural enterprise, but later admitted these thefts to the management because I had come to recognize the error of my ways. I then paid for the stolen goods. My Communist interlocutor then expressed the view that this was stupid of me, since my theft had weakened the capitalist system, and was therefore a praiseworthy action. In his terminology, a clear case of theft was transformed into a justifiable action in the class struggle.

According to a recent survey by the American Council on Education, three-quarters of the young people who take up university studies in America believe that the main purpose in life is to get rich. Twenty years ago only 39 percent shared that view. A majority of the students covered by the survey are now going to a university to learn how to earn more money.

In its 8 September 1987 edition, the *Wall Street Journal* reported a survey of senior executives which showed that over half the persons questioned would adapt the rules of the business game to their own wishes. "Ethics are fine but they may be an obstacle and stand in the way of a successful career," was the prevailing opinion expressed by one interviewee. Another said, "I know of unethical actions at every level of our management but I have to behave in the same way if I am to survive."

For seven years, the Hertz car rental company billed artificially high repair costs to customers who had been involved in accidents. Forms and signatures were forged. Computer programs included exaggerated prices and double accounting figures for its customers. Thirteen million dollars flowed into the firm's accounts in this way, as an investigation by the Department of Justice showed; afterward, Hertz admitted the fraud and paid the damages. The surprising thing about all this is the fact that hundreds of employees of the Hertz organization throughout the country followed the instructions of ambitious and dishonest superiors with no apparent twinge of conscience in order to survive—just like we Germans under the Nazis. Only our stakes were higher.

Theft means taking something which belongs to another person and getting rich at the cost of someone else. Anyone who enriches himself at the cost of another is in fact stealing from him. If I make someone pay for something which is not worth the price, I am stealing his money. Clearly not just cupidity, but also theft are coming to be seen as normal in our society. However, this morally reprehensible behavior has been given the new and agreeable name of "good business sense." Theft and deception have assumed epidemic proportions in our financial institutions, according to the conclusion reached by a Congressional Committee of Enquiry in October 1988. But the investigators didn't see the real truth of the matter and believed that this state of affairs was attributable to inadequate controls!

This, though, is not true, as we know from James Ring Adams, who covered the banking crisis for the *Wall Street Journal, Barron's,* and *The American Spectator.* He looked into the details of the U.S. savings and loan debacle. Politicians under the leadership of Jim Wright had first passed the deposit insurance law, which forced the federal government (already deep in the red) to be guarantor for all deposits of up to one hundred thousand dollars, which was naturally applauded by most innocent depositors. This guarantee then was commercialized by Merril Lynch, among others, and money-greedy and unscrupulous financial experts ripped off the savings and loan institutions to the tune of billions since the government had to pay up. When the supervision began to smell the rot, influence peddling on Capitol Hill through "campaign contributions" managed to bring political influence to bear on procedures to neutralize uncompromising supervisors so that the rip-off could continue for some more years. Economists at Stanford University estimate the cost to the American taxpayers for the next forty years at $1,368 trillion, including $913 billion in interest—$5,472 for every person in the United States.

"High-flyers bent on plundering a thrift or bank," comments Adams, "had discovered that if they invest a small portion of their take in campaign contributions, they could buy enough political clout to keep the examiners off their backs for a year or two or five, long enough anyway to develop a 20, 50, to 100 million dollar scam. And, since to pocket one dollar they had to lend $20, the loss at a single corrupt thrift could easily exceed one billion dollars."[4]

Between 1980 and 1983, savings and loan failures had "criminal misconduct" as their principal cause in 25 percent of the cases, as one congressional survey stated. Failures between 1985 and 1987 had fraud in all of the cases. Congressional staff director Peter S. Barash explained the situation this way: "The United States government is now confronting a growing and long-term epidemic of insider and outsider abuse, misconduct, and criminality in financial institutions."[5] So far, I have not heard any government define its real problems by their proper names.

In the *Reader's Digest, Sports Car* magazine reporter Robert Sikorski explains how he serviced a second-hand car down to the last detail and then drove across the United States. He visited 225 auto shops. Before each visit, he simply detached a cable. He then asked the garage mechanics to ascertain and repair the damage. Fifty-six percent of the mechanics tried to mislead him, performed unnecessary work, sold unnecessary components, or billed work which had not been performed. Some even caused new damage, and others were just not interested in providing any service at all. Only 28 percent behaved correctly.

The U.S. auto mechanic shops are not alone. When I pick up my car at a service station in Mexico, I often have to take it to another on the next day in the generally vain hope that I may find someone who will do a professional job. At almost all the gasoline stations in Acapulco, I have seen how the meters are manipulated to make the consumer pay for gas which never reaches his tank. When my brother-in-law, Hans, and sister, Sibylle, came to visit us by car, they bought gas near Monterrey. Their car's tank has a twenty-gallon capacity. The "clever" pump attendant tried unsuccessfully to charge the "dumb gringos" for forty gallons.

I know of a married couple in Germany who have been receiving unemployment benefits for years, and moonlighting for just as long. They drive a Mercedes. When the period of entitlement to unemployment benefits is about to expire, the husband finds a job and works officially for a few weeks; he pays a few contributions before reverting to his former lucrative way of life. I therefore have my doubts that across-the-board extension of unemployment benefits could meet the personal and national requirements as they should.

According to a survey by Gordon Tullock, which he published in his 1983 book *Economics of Income Redistribution*, welfare assistance for each poor family of four persons in the United States costs forty-eight thousand dollars. In actual fact, the recipients get only between sixty-five hundred and eight thousand dollars. The rest is swallowed up by the administrative apparatus whose representatives grow rich on the taxpayer.

The U.S. subsidiary of Nestle, Beech-Nut Nutrition Corporation, sold flavored sugared water for many years labeled as apple juice for babies, with a price to match. In the Sheraton Gifts store near Times Square in New York, the proprietor persuaded me to buy three Persian carpets from him which I paid for on the spot. He then consigned to me three Pakistani carpets; their value was just one-tenth of that of the Persian carpets, but they looked similar. With the resolute assistance of my brother-in-law, I finally managed to right this "confusion."

About half a million unnecessary Caesarean sections were performed in 1986 by American doctors on expectant mothers, according to reports by Dr. Sidney Wolfe and his colleagues at Public Citizen Health Research Group in Washington. Not only does this increase the risk—Wolfe estimates that 140 women have died as a result of unnecessary Caesarean operations—it also boosts the income of the practitioners and hospitals: sixteen hundred dollars extra per birth. The extra cost to the health organizations and insurance companies in 1986 was estimated in this survey at $728 million. The state attorney's office in Philadelphia was investigating at the same time the cases of 400 doctors who were suspected of receiving illegal kickbacks from four medical laboratories in exchange for steering them patient labwork. At the same time, the public prosecutor's office in Germany was investigating the cases of 1,100 doctors and dentists who were accused of issuing false receipts which were presented to Social Security for payment.

In the United States, the attempt to claim compensation from others for reasons of every kind is so embedded in everyday life that not only the insurance business is in a state of crisis, but also cities, local authorities, and untold individuals have to live with the constant risk of finding their very existence threatened by complaints of one sort or another. American justice has thrown the door wide open to cupidity, and unscrupulous attorneys attach no importance whatever to society and to the moral justification of a legal action as long as they receive their lucrative share of the outpayments. John S. Tomkins writes on this subject in *Reader's Digest*: "Legal actions often spread an odor of cupidity. When something goes wrong, too many people look for someone to accuse as the culprit. The Americans have become the most litigious people in the world who are no longer willing to accept their own failings."

Once when we left our house unattended in Mexico for a weekend, we forgot to turn off a water tap. When we came back on Monday, the house was under water. The damage was extensive. Friends advised me to indicate the cause as the breakage of the water pipe, which was covered by our insurance, and offered to testify on our behalf. As I was short of cash, the temptation was considerable. Finally, I reported accurately to the insurance company what had in fact occurred, although I knew that water damage was not included in the insurance coverage. I was then pleasantly surprised when the insurance company did pay the damage in full without any comment. High insurance premiums are the consequence of the actions of millions of less-than-honest insured persons and doctors. Budget deficits due to escalating social benefits are the consequence of vote-hungry irresponsible lawmakers and of the dishonesty of millions who make false declarations or wish to be paid for doing nothing, a fact which makes the possibility of alleviating genuine need increasingly difficult.

Cupidity is the same in the north and south. The possibilities differ, but the substance is always the same. Consider the widespread allegations of corruption made against Arturo Durazo Moreno, the police chief of Mexico City in the years 1976 to 1982. His assistant for many years, Lt. Col. Jose Gonzalez, described in his best-seller *The Black Deeds of Black Durazo* his boss's sources of revenue, excluding only those accruing from the narcotics trade, which are difficult to prove or calculate. It would take up too much space to reproduce the entire list here. Durazo was not the original inventor, but an expert in the execution of a system, according to which the police districts were required to pay to him each month a share of the fines collected by them (without any receipt, of course); they were asked to collect these fines from motorists. Each traffic policeman had his quota, and there are extremely popular and highly lucrative intersections at which only carefully selected policemen were posted. Simply in wages for two thousand nonexistent policemen, which Durazo cashed from the city administration's payroll, he received the proud sum of 40 million pesos each month, equivalent at the then current exchange rate to $1.4 million. Extrapolated to the six years of his term of office, these items alone (Gonzalez lists sixteen in all) brought him close to $103 million. Naturally he also collected the uniforms of these nonexistent policemen and sold them again. He used real policemen as workers to construct his magnificent rural and seaside residences. The total of all his monthly revenue from these various items was more than 726 million pesos, equivalent to $25 million. For the seventy-two months of his six-year term of office, this gives 52 billion pesos or $1.87 billion. Whether these figures are altogether accurate is not the decisive factor. The scale of the payments is certainly correct. Like every Mexican, I contributed to this total and can confirm the substance of the story.

In comparison, it is interesting to note that the municipal budget of Mexico City for 1977 stood at a total of 23.5 billion pesos, less than half the total income of the "patriot" Durazo.

The then president of the Republic, Jose Lopez Portillo, not only may have covered up for his bosom friend, but it is said in Mexico that he certainly did not content himself with much less. Lopez Portillo has acquired the reputation of having been the country's most corrupt president, a reputation which cannot even be disputed by his predecessor, Luis Echevarria. At the end of his term of office, the latter was also one of the world's richest men. This did not, however, prevent him from constantly calling for a new world economic order in which the industrial nations, not he, would be required to shell out.

According to an estimation by the American author and journalist Sol Sanders, Lopez Portillo, as the elected president of Mexico, stole $3.5 billion in his six-year term of office between 1976 and 1982. In an article published in the *Washington Post* on 15 May 1984, Jack Anderson estimated that Lopez Portillo's successor, Miguel de la Madrid, had managed to divert into his own account between thirteen and fourteen million U.S. dollars in the first four months of his term of office, and $126 million by May 1984. Concurrently with these activities, both presidents played the tune of a permanent anti-corruption campaign and moral renewal. If we were to estimate the total of all that has been stolen or extorted by blackmail in the last four terms of office of Mexico's presidents and members of the government bureaucracy in these twenty-four years alone, we would arrive at astronomical figures; to put it cynically, a few billion are neither here nor there. There are rumors that Salinas de Gotary enriched himself during his term as president by $26 billion. He left his people and his country in shambles. I think these people are not just greedy; they are sick and amoral.

The Morgan Guarantee Bank, early in 1989, estimated the total capital which had been transferred out of Mexico at $85 billion, equivalent to 87.6 percent of the foreign debt then. This capital could have been used to develop the country and improve the standard of living, especially of ordinary Mexicans. Capital is diverted out of the country from two sources: first, by those who have no confidence in their own government, and second, by dishonest members of the government apparatus. With an honest government, Mexico could experience economic success on an untold scale.

In 1975, with the leader of the Jamaican opposition and financier, Edward Seaga, and his brother-in-law, my attorney Hugh Hart (who later was Jamaican mining and tourism minister), I visited Port au Prince in order to conclude an agreement with the Haiti government on a project in the city harbor. We wanted to reclaim part of the harbor and build a shopping center and residential complex there as the first step towards a new and attractive face for the capital. The project was ready and financing was available. After Seaga and Hart had already visited Haiti several times, the matter was now due to be concluded in a contract. We spent a whole day with several ministers and two hours with President Jean-Claude Duvalier ("Baby Doc"), who gave us his agreement and asked us to settle the last outstanding details with the ministers responsible. It then turned out that these details consisted of kickbacks, or to put it more elegantly, "commissions" for the ministers concerned, who wanted 20 percent of the project cost to go into their own pockets in advance.

A certain figure already had been included in our calculations for this purpose; as is the case almost everywhere in Latin America (with the exception of Chile), nothing moves without such commissions. But the project could not stand a 20 percent advance commission, and since the "patriots" insisted on it, that part of the harbor is still under water and the appearance of the capital remains as depressing as ever.

When I spoke with friends in India of the $3.5 billion diverted by Lopez Portillo into his own pocket, they seemed to think it was not very much; I might reasonably assume that the late Ferdinand E. Marcos, when president of the Philippines, likewise enriched himself during his term of office. Before Marcos became president in 1966, his total assets stood at thirty thousand dollars. At the end of his presidency, the wardrobe of the Marcos family far exceeded that of Salvador Allende, who had modestly refrained from installing gold-plated taps in his bathroom. Allende did not waste his time on religion either. Marcos, on the other hand, had a chapel in which the statues of saints were bedecked with jewels.

The temptation to grab what one can is the same for everyone even though the possibilities differ. Everyone can place limitations on himself by attempting to satisfy the needs of others. Anyone can do this; anyone who at the very least has a real-life neighbor, since I am not speaking about the abstract neighbor of all mankind. It would be particularly interesting to compile statistics showing, for example, what the legislators who set up the most generous social programs using other people's money, including the money of future generations, in fact do with their own personal revenue.

I very much doubt whether the same generosity to others prevails in the private sphere. Because of this lack of realism, the budgets of most countries are well on the way to uncontrollable chaos. The Koran says that "he who overcomes cupidity within himself will prosper."

I, too, would like to be rich, but I have sworn to myself not to grow rich at the cost of others and not to close my eyes to the needs of other people. I proved that in my factory in Mexico, an account of which I give in my book *Connecting with the Power of God*. Money does not serve only to maintain our own standard of living and for our own capital formation, but gives us a possibility to improve the lives of others and to finance tasks important for society. No person and no nation can serve money and God at the same time. It is one or the other.

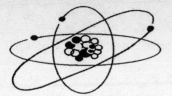

The Not-So-Dead Communism

Communism is dead; democracy has prevailed and is being established in Eastern Europe. The totalitarian Communist system has broken down and the Soviet Union has disappeared; the former Communists are now learning the ropes of capitalism. The Cold War is over; we have won. So we describe the present situation as the post-Cold War era and disarm rapidly.

But what are the facts? First of all, there are 1.2 billion people still forced to live in the official Communist-totalitarian states of China, North Korea, Vietnam, Laos, Cambodia, and Cuba. As the *Wall Street Journal* recently pointed out, that is as many people as the combined populations of Western Europe, the United States of America, Canada, Latin America, and Japan. It was the Chinese Communist leaders who said thirty years ago: "We believe that atomic war is not only inevitable but necessary for the triumph of Communism, and we are willing to lose 300 million lives." Naturally, they mean the lives of others, not their own. Their system is still very much in place. They are still the same people, and their philosophy is not dead. The Communist leaders are well on the way to making China (with our help) the biggest economy and probably the most powerful military force on earth within the next thirty years. In addition to their own hardware, they also have access to the military technology of the Soviets.

The Former Soviet Union

It is true that the Soviet Union, the leading Communist state, fell apart. But out of the Soviet Union came eleven successor-states, not counting the Baltic countries, which are all governed by Communists. Communists were thus able to add eight seats to the three they already had in the United Nations for a total of eleven—not bad for a bankrupt philosophy. This pushed the democratic states of law in the United Nations deeper into a minority position. When Communist leaders in the former Soviet Union now sing to the tune of nationalism instead of Marxism-Leninism, it does not necessarily mean that their basic ideological world view has changed. All presidents in the Republics of the former Soviet Union are old Communist apparatchiks (members of a Communist party) and so are most of the members of parliament. The only non-Communist among them was Tsviyad Gamazakhurdiya, who was elected with 87 percent of the votes to be president of Georgia. He was accused of being a dictator and ousted by military force, instigated by President Eduardo Schevardnaze who, before becoming foreign minister of the Soviet Union, was Georgian minister of Interior, KGB boss, and general secretary of the Communist party of Georgia. In those days Schevardnaze was considered a specialist in refined methods of torture. Gamazakhurdiya, son of a famous poet and dissident, had been jailed by Schevardnaze because he brought out a documentation on torture in the prisons of Georgia.

The Russian armed forces are still a kind of state in themselves, and with their nuclear arsenal will remain a threat for a long time. Even though the danger of a frontal attack on Central Europe is not a very realistic possibility, the northern and southern European flanks, Norway and Turkey, remain exposed to unpleasant surprises. The sale of weapons to China, Iran, Libya, and others bring the desperately needed hard currency. The KGB, the equivalent to the Nazi Gestapo, has been reorganized but operates with the same number of five hundred thousand professionals, strengthened by additions from the former Eastern European intelligence and state security agencies. The Russian state security minister, Barannikow, as well as his deputy,

Oleinikor, have been with the KGB since the sixties, when the organization was still called MVD. The chief of foreign espionage, Primakov, has been at his job since 1957. In 1992, Barannikow refused a request from a visiting delegation of three Western intelligence services to give them his documentation on the East German State Security (STASI). No information has been rendered on the drug war against the United States and Europe by the Soviet government, waged under the control of the KGB for more than three decades. It is therefore safe to assume that the labels have changed in what used to be the Soviet Union, but that the fundamentals remain the same.

And what happened to the fortune of $180 billion of the Soviet Communist party which disappeared, together with 350 tons of gold, shortly before Gorbachev resigned as general secretary? Or to the $30 billion, which in 1992 (according to the managing director of the International Monetary Fund, Michel Camdessus) was siphoned off to foreign accounts by members of the KGB and the Nomenclatura? This amounts to considerable sums for which the West is requested to compensate. It should be obvious to everyone that what Russia needs in the first place is not money for the government, but people with character.

Germany

A similar pattern could be observed in East Germany. According to Ferdinand Kroh, a German political analyst, 3,300 objects and real estate properties with a value of approximately $38 billion were transferred into "private" property shortly before reunification, the new private owners being members of the STASI and the Communist Nomenclatura. The transfers were facilitated by the last two DDR governments of Communist Modrow and fellow traveller de Maiziere. Some attempts to transfer huge sums of money to foreign accounts have been intercepted, but others probably were successful. Orders CFS 43 and CFS 44 of 7 December 1989, signed by STASI General Wolfgang Schwanitz, detail the procedures to take over STASI property and cover up all tracks. Journalists Manfred Schell and Werner Kalinka, who investigated the STASI, wrote, "The question arises whether the STASI developed a survival strategy long before the East German state crumbled."[1] There was no take-over master plan prepared in Bonn. Hans Schwenke, one of those appointed by the German government to supervise the dissolution of the STASI, concludes that "the fast entry of the DDR into the Federal Republic was prepared far in advance, long before the people on the streets adopted that desire." STASI personnel took the cream of East German assets and left the rest to the German taxpayer, including myself. There is a well-equipped Fifth Column in Germany. There are also now thirty Communists in the German Bundestag, which we have never had before. Communism is not dead in Germany.

Nicaragua

Nor is it dead in Cuba, China, or South Africa, to name only a selected number of other countries. In this context we'll now have a look at Nicaragua. I was there at the end of the eighties when the Sandinistas were in power, and I went back to Managua in October 1992. My findings were disquieting. To put the conclusion at the beginning, I consider Pres. Violeta Chamorro to be a democratic window-dressing for the Communist Sandinistas, who continue to hold the real power in Nicaragua. It is a disgraceful betrayal to the people who voted for democracy and brought her into the presidential palace. I fully concur with the excellent Republican staff report "Nicaragua Today" to the Committee on Foreign Relations United States Senate of August 1992, which details the abuses of the Chamorro government. Further documentation was provided to me by the Nicaraguan Association for Human Rights, whose workers and their families live under the constant threat of assassination by those forces whose immorality they expose. The reason for this democratic farce, I believe, is the fact that the Sandinistas, since the beginning of the demise of the Eastern European Communist states, had no more access to any finances, without which government operation neither then nor today is viable. They had to adopt a style which pleased the dumb Western democrats. The calculation proved to be correct. Right after the "democratic victory," money poured into the country to the tune of hundreds of millions of dollars, most of it borrowed from banks, of course, by Western governments who in turn can rely on their working population and taxpayers—no strings attached. Capitalists don't know anything about communism. Communists, however, know everything about capitalism and capitalists.

Violeta Chamorro does not appear to govern for the people who elected her to the office of president and have the majority in Parliament. She seems to govern *against* the people with the support of a parliamentary coalition of the Sandinistas and ten deserters of her own party, the Democratic Union, whom she bought, according to the Republican Staff Report, with the major part of one million dollars—money which was stolen from European assistance funds. The Nicaraguan controller-general accused Antonio Lacayo, her son-in-law and chief of staff, of committing this theft—and others—but the controller-general was powerless to proceed with criminal charges.

Antonio Lacayo governed the country together with Gen. Humberto Ortega, who was and is commander of the armed forces, which, like the police, remain Sandinistan. Ortega should stand trial for the atrocities he is said to have ordered or committed. People now speak of a government coalition of the two. Not answered is the question, Who holds the real power, Daniel Ortega, the former president, or his brother Humberto? In any case, as strapped as Nicaragua is for funds, there was enough left for Humberto in 1991 to send $1 million monthly to his private account in Canada. The account number was broadcast by CNN. The monthly payments went down to five hundred thousand dollars—during 1992. Lenin Cerna, former commandant of the infamous Sandinistan central prison El Chipote, now serves as chief of intelligence for Mrs. Chamorro and the army. He is responsible for multiple murders and tortures like the worst of our concentration camp commandants. Neither he nor any of his accomplices were put on trial. When Chamorro speaks of reconciling the country, her words are questionable. You cannot reconcile with unrepenting criminals.

Sixty of the Sandinista leaders live in stolen houses. Additionally, fourteen Sandinist organizations occupy houses taken away from their owners. Precisely as it happened in East Germany at the end of the Communist rule, the Sandinista government made "legal" arrangements shortly before turning over power to Mrs. Chamorro, so that they could appear as owners of the houses they already occupied illegally. They also grabbed 25 percent of the country's fertile arable land. Everybody in Nicaragua knows the facts; they call them "Piñata." But after three years of her presidency, Mrs. Chamorro has made no serious effort to restore the stolen properties to their rightful owners, which include quite a few Americans.

The Contras demobilized according to the peace agreement and delivered their arms to the authorities. The army did not demobilize as it was supposed to according to the same agreement, but simply shifted soldiers with their arms to reserve units, thus giving the appearance of reduction in the armed forces. The Contras were delivered helpless to the mercy of their deadly enemies by the United Nations and Western expert peacemakers. Until October 1992, a total of 217 Contras had been murdered, among them twelve commanders. These assassinations were frequently committed in broad daylight—most of the killers or their army units being known and documented. None of the assassinators was brought to justice. The most spectacular assassination was the one of top Contra commander Enrique Bermudez, who was shot and killed in the parking lot of the Intercontinental Hotel.

This pattern of how to liquidate the opposition was established by Lenin. It happened in many countries, and right now can be observed in Angola, where the same fate was prepared for Contra leader Jonas Savimbi. In October 1992, the Communist government party, the Popular Movement for the Liberation of Angola of President Jose Eduardo dos Santos (MLPA), invited Jonas Savimbi, leader of the Union for the Total Independence of Angola (UNITA), with a delegation to Luanda for peace talks. Savimbi excused himself in the last minute, but nine top generals and brigadiers came. They were immediately shot dead. Government soldiers then slaughtered ten to twenty thousand UNITA soldiers and supporters. A number of Western reporters, including several from Washington, were present. Did they report on this? Of course not. Instead, Savimbi, like Buthelezi in South Africa, is being portrayed by these reporters as an obstacle to peace. That should make the reader of this think. He might begin to realize how the Socialists in the media, and in his government, lie to him and brainwash him as adeptly as Joseph Goebbels, the master of the lie and the art of manipulation.

But, back to Nicaragua. Five of the nine members of the Nicaraguan Supreme Court are Sandinistas. President Chamorro does not appoint others even though she could. The Sandinistas also control the unions and the bureaucracy under the level of vice-minister. Sixty of the seventy radio channels and three of the four television stations are in the hands of the Sandinistas or the government. The Chamorro family controls practically all newspapers. The president's youngest son, Carlos Fernando, has been for many years the editor in chief of the *Barricada*, the official organ of the Sandinista party. Daughter Christiana, wife of Antonio Lacayo, is president of *La Prensa*, a famous newspaper known for standing up to Somoza and the Sandinistas during their respective rules. *La Prensa* is not the same newspaper anymore. Pedro Joaquin, Jr., with whom I talked in his newspaper office, is not a Sandinista, but I do not think that he and his colleagues seriously challenge his mother. Finally, *El Nuevo Diario*, a mass circulation tabloid, is owned by Xavier Chamorro, the president's brother-in-law.

The people of Nicaragua, who voted for democracy, are being led down the garden path by a bunch of gangsters. They see the impertinence of the Sandinistas, the lack of justice, the opportunism of the government, and how their dreams are being shattered. The result is growing nihilism, which pervades society like poison. Not all is lost, though. There are men and women fighting, like Cardinal Archbishop Ovando Bravo, Vice President Godoy, and the former president of Parliament, Cesar, among others. Communism is not dead in Nicaragua.

Cuba

Nor is it dead in Cuba. They had an "election" there at the beginning of 1993. What a joke: There was only one candidate and no one else to vote for. The misery today is far worse than in 1987 when I visited the country. Castro has no money since his friend Gorbachev left office, so he asks the people to sacrifice for socialism. The need for the people to sacrifice seems to be a universal feature independent of economic system or political organization. But I consider the mental, spiritual, and intellectual poverty of the population even more terrible than their physical misery.

The most disgusting part of Castro's evil character, his human baseness, is most clearly apparent in his treatment of his friends and fellow fighters whom he deceived just as he deceived world public opinion when he portrayed himself initially as a Democrat and non-Communist. Castro lied to them about his intentions as long as he needed them to get into power; once there he didn't care. When he dropped his mask, many of the revolutionary leaders turned against him. They were mercilessly excluded, eliminated, or imprisoned: commanders Huber Matos, Clodomino Miranda, Eloy Gutierrez Menoyo, Jesus Carreras, Pacoi Almoina, Claudio Medel, Rafael de Pino, and Mario Chavez, to name only a few.

Castro seems to have revelled in the suffering of his victims, just as Hitler did. Armando Valladares, who spent twenty-two years in Cuban prisons because he stood up to Castro, describes in his book *Against all Hope* the suffering of prisoners in detail. One chapter of his book is entitled "A Nazi Prison in the Caribbean." He is referring to Boniato prison in the eastern region of the island, where cruel biological and psychological experiments were carried out on prisoners in the same way as those organized in Nazi Germany by SS leader Heinrich Himmler. Soviet, East German, Czech, and Hungarian experts in torture had pooled their scientific know-how to build this complex (with its cells specially designed for specific forms of torture) in which experiments were conducted on detainees with the aim of breaking down mental resistance through physical terror.

Prisoners have spent weeks and months in darkened cells living in their own excrement as though in a latrine, with no possibility of washing. They also went without proper food, were unable to move, were in oven-like heat in the summer without drinking water, and in some cases were naked for years on end. It was part of the daily routine, and probably still is, for the guards to beat defenseless prisoners with iron bars wrapped in rubber tubing, chains, and electrical cables; to kick them in the kidneys and soft part of the body until they were left alone in their cells, bleeding and unconscious, often with their teeth and bones broken, only to be subjugated to a repetition of this treatment the very next day. And these were no isolated occurrences, but rather a planned, continuing routine.

Valladares, who was released after twenty-two years because of the ceaseless efforts of his wife to mobilize public opinion and Western government leaders, is a shining example of a man who does not deliver his soul but would rather die than betray his truth. When the commandant of La Cabana prison, Lt. Justo Hernandez de Medina, drew his attention to material progress—obviously existing only in his imagination—Valladares told him, "Even if you were to attain a higher standard of living than any capitalist country and every kind of product was available in abundance, I should still be an opponent of your system, because it denies men their freedom, not because there are no consumer goods. Progress of the revolution to which you refer is therefore meaningless to me."[2] Armando Valladares became an American citizen and U.S. ambassador to the Human Rights Commission of the United Nations.

When evaluating the situation that the people of Cuba are in today, one has to remember how Fidel Castro came into power in the first place. According to Earl E.T. Smith, who was U.S. ambassador to Cuba from 1957 to 1959, the ones responsible for the rise to power of the Communists in Cuba were those on the fourth floor of the State Department and the liberal press in America. On the fourth floor, Smith explained in his book with the same name, decisions concerning Latin America were made. These policymakers brought down Batista, an "evil dictator," by cutting any support to his government and pushing other governments to do the same, while at the same time the liberal press portrayed Fidel Castro as a progressive, non-Communist reformer.

Smith testified in 1960 before a subcommittee of the United States Senate, and after listing the various actions taken by the U.S. government to isolate Batista, such as cancelling arms deliveries, he said:

> I believe that the policies are determined in the lower echelon, and by the time the higher echelon receives them, policies have already been made, and they have to live by them. . . . The Secretary of State was preoccupied with Peking, Moscow, and Berlin. Policy decisions on Cuban affairs were determined on the Fourth Floor of the State Department, where influential persons believed in the revolution and hoped for its success. So far as I know, no definite policy governing our attitude to the friendly government of Cuba was set on the fifth floor (the top echelon of the State Department). The Secretary of State did not, during my entire mission, discuss the Cuban problem with me.[3]

The president at that time was Dwight Eisenhower, and his secretary of state was John Foster Dulles.

Herbert L. Matthews wrote glowing articles in the *New York Times* about changes the revolutionaries in the Sierra Madre were going to bring to the people of Cuba who were suffering at the hands of the corrupt dictator, Batista. It may be enough to quote one paragraph from his first article on Cuba, published by the *New York Times* on Sunday, 24 February 1957:

> Fidel Castro and his 26th of July Movement are the flaming symbol of his opposition to the regime. The organization, which is apart from the university students' opposition, is formed of youth of all kinds, it is a revolutionary movement that calls itself socialistic. It is also nationalistic, which generally in Latin America means anti-Yankee. The program is vague and couched in generalities, but it amounts to a new deal in Cuba, radical, democratic and therefore anti-Communist. The real core of its strength is that it is fighting against the military dictatorship of President Batista.

The same tenor could be read in dozens of other newspapers.

The same pattern, a combined effort to install Communist regimes in other countries by the lower echelon of the State Department and the liberal media, can be observed in the battle for South Africa, which I shall describe in detail in another chapter. Communism is not dead in the United States of America.

The Drug War

"Estimates of the money U.S. citizens paid for illegal drugs in the early 1980s ranged from $80 to $110 billion per year," writes Dr. Joseph D. Douglass in 1990, "with another $60 billion spent on associated health costs. Since those estimates were made, the estimates have doubled; the total yearly cost today within the United States may rival the $300 billion budget of the Department of Defense. The global cost of drug trafficking may exceed $500 billion per year. Some estimates run as high as $1 trillion per year."[4]

Douglass, a national security affairs expert, describes in detail in his book *Red Cocaine—The Drugging of America* how the Soviet strategy to destroy the moral fiber of American society unfolds and how the United States government fails to address the issue. He received an important part of his information from Gen. Maj. Jan Sejna, whom I quote and refer to in another context in this book. Sejna was a member of the Czechoslovakian Central Committee of the Communist party, a member of Parliament and its presidium, first party secretary at the ministry of defense (where he was also chief of staff), and a member of the Minister's Kolegium. Apart from other central administrative positions, Sejna was secretary of the Defense Council, the top decision-making body in matters of defense, foreign policy, intelligence, and economy. He was a central player in the establishment of the structures for the unfolding drug war and represented Czechoslovakia in the meetings with the Soviet Security Council. Sejna defected in 1968.

Mao Tse-tung began using drugs for political purposes back in 1928. The Soviets jumped on the bandwagon in the fifties. At the end of 1955, the Soviet Defense Council approved the guidelines for the drug war against the United States, and in 1962 Khrushchev made it official government policy for all Eastern European countries as well. He made the schools priority targets so as to corrupt the future leaders of the enemy country and stressed the need to undermine the American work ethic, pride, and loyalty with drugs. "Anything that speeds the destruction of capitalism is moral," he declared.[5] Tanks were only needed, he emphasized, after deception and disinformation campaigns had been successful and the destruction of the moral fiber of capital-ist society had advanced satisfactorily.

Decisions were always made on the level of first secretaries, prime ministers, ministers of defense, and chiefs of general staff of East Bloc countries. The strategy, though, was executed in such a way that the Soviet Union did not appear anywhere, even though the KGB was controlling every detail, and the intelli-gence services of the satellites were the actors. The Cuban, and later the Sandinistan governments, were given key roles. The instruction for all was to infiltrate and take over existing drug operations on the level of distribution as well as of production, establish when necessary new operations, infiltrate and use orga-nized crime, train terrorists, and combine all in a deadly assault on American society. According to Soviet estimates, by 1967 they were in control of 37 percent of drug production for the supply in the U.S. and Canadian markets and of 31 percent of the distribution network. It is safe to assume that by 1990 the Soviets were the majority player in the field.

Scientists and medical doctors from the Central Military Hospital and the Airforce Scientific Center in Prague were engaged since the beginning of the sixties in the development of biological and chemical warfare agents, mind control drugs, and more effective narcotics. Their knowledge was later passed on to their Cuban counterparts, who in turn specialized in drugs, which led to "intellectual stagnation." The Cubans also were assigned the task of organizing a training program for blacks and a pro-duction and distribution system in the Caribbean to attack Ameri-can inner cities with blacks. The objective was to create political instabilities by fostering resentments in the black communities, especially in the unemployed, because of economic inequalities, a program named eco-racism. The rationale for pushing drugs into this group was that crime and the general erosion of West-ern moral values would be stimulated because the use of drugs destroys judgment and leads people into crime, homosexuality, and other immoral activities.

Crack, a new drug with a low price targeting low-income people and students, appeared on the market in 1986. "Crack is a highly potent form of cocaine that is smoked," explains

Douglass. "It enters the blood stream through the lungs and proceeds immediately to the brain. It can be almost instantly addictive, gives the user a sense of self-confidence and superiority, and is closely linked with violent behaviour."[6] While it cannot be proven in which laboratory the drug was created, the professional and well-orchestrated market penetration by blacks from Jamaica and Haiti, especially in the inner cities, points in the direction of the Soviets, who two decades earlier had laid down the strategy which appears now to be extraordinarily successful in bringing a free society to its knees.

The most astounding feature in this whole affair is the reluctance or inability of American and other Western governments to address the true nature of drug warfare until today. What has the CIA been doing? There is evidence that the State Department and the CIA have for years suppressed the information General Sejna brought to the West. The State Department is actively engaged in supporting undemocratic and Communist movements like the South African National Congress and the SWAPO in Namibia. The foreign policy of the leading Western power, from which the European governments take their cues, is directed by men who are opposed to a free and democratic society, who betray the best interest of their country on behalf of those who attack us.

I consider it out of the question that the drug war was abandoned because of the demise of the Soviet Union. The Cubans and the Sandinistas alone would probably be capable of continuing it on their own. But, the silence of the KGB makes it obvious, I believe, that they continue their business as usual. Furthermore, since the drug business is highly profitable, it is very unlikely that the amoral representatives of bankrupt countries could turn their backs on such an income. Communism is not dead in Russia.

Definitions of Communist, Fellow Traveller, and Marxism-Leninism

The bearer of the Communist philosophy is a Communist—but not exclusively. There are millions of people who do not call themselves Communists or think of themselves as Com-

munists but who live partially or totally by the Communist philosophy. They are moral and ideological "fellow travellers," and
you can find them in every government around the world. Are
Socialists and liberals Communists? Is Gorbachev perhaps just
a clever Communist? Let's try to define what a Communist is.
What are his motives, his ethics, his purposes? What makes him
tick? Do the disappearance of totalitarian structures and rules in
some countries, and the bankruptcy of the Socialist economies,
produce the kind of new person who did not emerge from their
system as Karl Marx had predicted? In other words, have the
millions of Communists and especially the hard-core
nomenclatura around the world ceased to be Communists and
become Democrats, accepting and applying democratic rules?
Are they now different people from what they were five years
ago? I think it would be very naive and dangerous to believe this.

Start with what Communists are not. They are not economists who believe in state-owned, centrally controlled economies. The belief that capitalism has defeated communism is
about the dumbest thing one could think of. The idea of ownership of the means of production by the people was indeed a
theoretical concept in the framework of a social and economic
philosophy in the perverted mind of Karl Marx. But in the
practices of the last decades in the Socialist states it became an
instrument for the enrichment of the nomenclatura and their
control of the people, precisely in the same way as government
bureaucracies in America and elsewhere conduct themselves. The
difference is relative. When Nelson Mandela wants to national-
ize part of the South African economy, as he continues to say,
it has nothing to do with economy or justice. He and his crew
just want to put their hands on income for themselves without
having to work for it. I know this system from Latin America,
and to my surprise I found the same in the United States. That
is probably the reason why Mandela has so many friends in
Washington.

A Communist is selfish; he is a person who serves his own
power and that of his comrades and has no regard for moral
values, opinions, and the rights of others. He hides his overriding purpose behind social phrases, using the mistakes and weak-

nesses of others to cover up what he is really after and making his immoral acts appear to be a justified reaction to their misdeeds. Joseph Goebbels, Hitler's minister of propaganda, was a master at this. People remained spellbound after listening to him—but his and his comrade's actions did not match their words. Do you know any people like that? Envying and hating those who are better off, belonging to a privileged group from which one is excluded, or just yielding power to which one aspires are central in the Communist-Socialist motivation. The rich—plutocrats as Hitler called them (who can be individuals or countries)—are always the others who are being blamed and called up to pay, sometimes with their lives, sometimes with what is politely called a "fair contribution." Hidden is the determination in a Communist-Socialist, born from envy, to steal the property of others, by force if necessary, in order to live the good life oneself. Naturally this is not called theft but expropriation or taxes. The reality of massive theft could be found in each one of the East European countries, as well as in Nicaragua.

Marxism-Leninism is a technique of ruthlessly taking over power and keeping it with whatever means are necessary. Not only murder but character assassination of opponents also play an important role. Truth is distorted and appetites for the properties of others are stimulated by establishing scapegoats. The resentments of all those who have been treated unjustly are mobilized against a given target. Any person with unresolved resentments within himself or ambitious appetites can be manipulated, and that is the simple answer to the question of why non-Communists over decades keep executing Communist policies. That was the key to the success of Eudocio Ravines in Chile, which I will describe in another chapter.

The Leninist global conspiracy consists in the first place of an invisible network of envious, power-hungry, and hate-filled people who share a resentment against God and society. Partly, I believe, this network was guided and organized by Moscow. But even if this Soviet organizational structure, basically provided by the KGB, no longer exists today—which is not certain, as I explained—this group of like-minded, negative people continues to have devastating effects on our society. It is human nature to try to justify one's own attitudes and actions. This justification cannot come from within a Communist since immorality opposes God's truth instilled in all of us and can be achieved only by getting everybody around to adhere to the same godless principles so that one becomes part of a generally accepted pattern of behavior and feels secure. Communism, like nazism, is, above all, an amoral social force bent on destroying absolute moral values, pulling everyone down to its own low moral level.

Obviously not everyone who is engaged in this kind of behavior and activity is a Communist, but he is a natural ally even if he considers himself to be an anti-Communist, indispensable to the advancement of totalitarian power. Anti-communism, it follows, is only a reaction (and an insufficient one) to evil action, which battles on the surface but does not attempt to cure the underlying evil. Lenin was an utterly amoral and ruthless person, a killer, a cheater, a liar, a mass murderer, and no less evil than Hitler. And so was Mao Zedong. They left us a heritage that will take generations to eliminate.

Let's also attempt to define the characteristics of an ideological "fellow traveller." Every person who belittles communism and believes he is not a Communist, yet furthers communism and Communist causes, falls into this category. The low level of American liberal journalism was made clear to me many years ago, at a time when Gorbachev's popularity began to rise. I still see Peter Jennings in an ABC studio, which was all draped in red with hammer and sickles all over the place, both hands in his pockets, explaining to his audience that after Stalin and his successors had mutilated the original humane ideas of Marx and Lenin, now Gorbachev had arrived on the scene to restore the battle for justice, for which the founders of communism had strived. Jennings doesn't know it, but he and those like him poison the minds of millions with lies, and the KGB disinformation department could not do it better if they tried.

John Barron summarizes Lenin's contribution to the history of mankind in the following terms:

> When Lenin lay dying after a succession of strokes in 1924, he had already defined the outline of future Soviet

society. He left the Russian people with an oligarchical dictatorship, a privileged class which is totally dependent on a political secret police and terror as the mainstay of dictatorship. Concentration camps, arrests on the grounds of membership in certain classes of society, sentences and executions without trial, enforced confessions for show trials, a system of informers and the concept of merciless mass terror were not introduced by Stalin but by Lenin. The terror which fell into disrepute decades later under the name of Stalinism was no more than pure Leninism practiced on a gigantic and maniacal scale.[7]

Since Gorbachev claims to be a Marxist-Leninist, the reader now knows what he stands for. There are plenty of his kind in the United Nations and the Security Council, whom we want to make the final authorities in this world. They go out by the front door and return through the back door.

"We stand for organized terror," explained Dzerzhinski, who, on instruction of Lenin, founded on 20 December 1917 the KGB, then called Tcheka. "The Tcheka has the task of defending the revolution and destroying its opponents."[8] That disdain of truth and of other people, which expresses itself in many different forms, is the real evil empire.

Dimitri Manuilsky, secretary general of the Communist International from 1946 to 1953, founding delegate, and the first Ukrainian ambassador to the United Nations with the task of transforming that body into an instrument of international class warfare to make it an operating base for the KGB, said the following in 1949 at the Moscow cadre-training school:

> Today we are not yet strong enough to attack. Our hour will strike in a few years. To win, we have to have recourse to the element of surprise. There is the need to lull the bourgeoisie. We shall unfold the most unprecedented peace movement that ever existed. There will be sensational rapprochement and unheard-of concessions. Befuddled and decadence-gripped capitalist states will be happy to cooperate with us in the interest of their own liquidation. We shall snatch at the opportunity to befriend them. As soon as they relax their vigilance we shall destroy them with our iron fist.

"Befuddled and decadence-gripped"—there is no better description of Western societies and of the mental condition of their leaders today. Dimitri Manuilsky erred in his timing but not in the substance of the unfolding drama. The peace and befriending phase is well advanced.

The Struggle for Chile

The struggle for Chile is a textbook example of the pursuit over several decades of long-term objectives by the Soviets and of the aimless, self-satisfied dilettantism of Western governments, which turn themselves into the executive organs of the attempt to instill immoral socialism in other countries.

On instructions from Moscow, Eudocio Ravines, the founder of the Peruvian Communist party, orchestrated the world's first Popular Front in the mid-thirties in Chile—an achievement rivalled only by the French. The idea of the People's Front was first developed by Henri Barbusse, a French author, friend of Stalin, and mentor of the Communist International. It is a tactic by which a resolute minority is able to attain power in a particular country through a phased operation, exploiting all the rules of the democratic game. In exchange for supporting a left-wing bourgeois candidate for the office of president and his party friends in parliamentary elections, the helpers (a small band of Communists) are given jobs and favors if the operation is successful. This enables them to subsequently expand their role, exert an influence on decisions, and exclude opponents until they are finally able to take over the structures of government. This is not achieved through democratic elections but by their absolute resolve to attain power and their skill in deceiving and manipulating other men, infiltrating democratic institutions and parties and misusing them to consolidate their own power.

Salvador Allende almost succeeded in the efforts which had been underway for thirty-five years. Those who took the crown from him have incurred the bitter enmity and lust for revenge of powerful international interests and poisoners of human minds.

I met Ravines in the early 1960s. He was small in stature. Behind his glasses his eyes sparkled and missed nothing; he used lively gestures to emphasize his comments, which reflected his thinking with great clarity and honesty. He was born in 1897 in Cajamarca, a small provincial capital in Northern Peru not far from the harbor town of Chiclayo.

Ravines grew up in bitter poverty. The great landowners, descendants of the Spanish conquistadores, were the kings to whose tune everyone danced. He became embittered and, even as a youth, began to rebel against the "hard and infamous reality," as he called it, against

> the regime of slavery, the miserable existence of degrad-
> ing poverty which it brought in its train, the deep-rooted
> injustice at the heart of this system. These landowners
> pronounced fine speeches about social justice but obliged
> even women and children to work for them without pay-
> ment whenever they so wished. In addition, they took a
> tithe on the harvest of the small peasants, forced them to
> milk the cows of the big landowners and even sheared
> their sheep. There was no one to oppose this behavior, no
> judges, no human forces, no divine court.[1]

When Ravines finally came to Lima as a young man, he joined the Left-leaning intellectual circle of author Jose Carlos Mariategui, to which Victor Raul Haya de la Torre, the former student and later founder of the Peruvian once-governing party, the APRA (Alianza Popular Revolucionaria Americana), be-longed. Ravines remained in close contact with Haya de la Torre in the years which followed. From Buenos Aires, where he be-gan to work with the Bureau of the Comintern (the Communist International), he went to Paris and Berlin and eventually reached Moscow. He stayed in Paris and Berlin with Haya de la Torre, who was visibly impressed by the Nazis, their methods, proces-sions, and flags, but decided to go his own way; however, he did not renounce the methods of the Nazis and the Soviets. Ravines in turn believed that Marx had found an explanation for the injustice in the world and that the Communist International pointed the way to justice. In the course of his career, he spent several periods in prison, was frequently expelled from his country, and took part in the Spanish Civil War.

In Moscow the concept of the Popular Front was then hammered out in week-long discussions in which many of the key Soviet and international leaders of the Comintern took part, such as Zinoviev, Bukharin, Radek, Kamenev, Thorez, Togliatti, Pieck, Kuessinen, Mao Tse-Tung, Gottwald, and Bela Kun. The Comintern was split in two directions: one led by Dimitri Manuilsky who advocated armed insurrection, the other under Georgi Dimitrov who wanted to follow the nonviolent path of the Popular Front; but their aim was the same—to seize power. There is no fundamental difference between "reformer" and "hardliner."

However, they were not just interested in Brazil and Chile, the two countries of immediate concern, but in the whole of Latin America and indeed in other countries beyond its borders. This aim was furthered by the presence of the leaders of the Latin American Soviet columns, Luis Carlos Prestes from Brazil, Vicente Lombardo Toledano from Mexico, Las Roca and Calendaria from Cuba, and Vittorio Cordovila from Argentina. Dimitrov made it clear that the Chilean experience was to serve as a textbook example for worldwide Soviet operations. Both Dimitri Manuilsky and Dimitrov had been presidents of the Comintern for many years. Dimitrov was secretary general of the Bulgarian Communist party and later the Bulgarian Premier. He became famous in 1933 when Hitler accused him of setting fire to the German Reichstag. Dimitri Manuilsky represented the Soviet Union at the founding meeting of the United Nations in San Francisco and was the first Ukrainian delegate. Acting on instructions from Stalin, he successfully internationalized the Popular Front tactic with a view to turning this organization, with the help of financial resources provided by the Western democracies, into an instrument of Soviet foreign policy and a base for KGB operations in the Americas. The process proved somewhat slower than expected but went ahead just the same.

In 1934, a compromise was arrived at in Moscow. An armed insurrection was to be incited in Brazil and the Popular Front tried in Chile. The Brazilian adventure led by Prestes was a bloody failure. The Chilean experiment under Ravines proved a resounding success which even converted Dimitri Manuilsky. Stalin dubbed the philosophy of the Popular Front the "Yenan Way"—a reference to a tactical experiment by the Chinese in Yenan. He instructed Ravines, via Barbusse, to meet with and take lessons from Chinese leaders Mao Tse-Tung, Chu Teh, and Li Li-sang, who were then in Moscow.

In his book *The Yenan Way*, Ravines reports on the content of these conversations. Li Li-sang explained,

> We can exploit the ambition of thousands of politicians of all statures, but especially the petty bourgeois, men who have not been able to attain the high positions to which they aspire, because their ambitions exceed their capabilities. If we, the communists, help them with large or small forces, they will join our camp not as party members but as our servants. They will find it worth their while to serve us. We won over hundreds of Chiang Kai-shek's officers in this way. The Chinese soldier is ambitious. He is power hungry, unlike his European counterparts and lusts after wealth, comfort and luxury. . . . By serving the ambition of these generals, we won advantages for the communists and gained positions which we could never have won by battle. Battles do not necessarily bring political victories. The Yenan way, which moves forward like a serpent, leads to great triumphs. The talent of the communists resides in knowing how to exploit those advantages.[2]

Ravines goes on to quote Mao Tse-tung:

> Our experience, the experience of the Yenan way is this: Men such as doctors, generals, dentists, mayors and lawyers who are not rich, love power not so much for its own sake and even less for the good that they can do with it. They want power because of the prosperity which it brings. As soon as they acquire power, they begin, like Napoleon, to demand money, money and more money. . . . Today they can really become rich. We shall soon be able to expropriate everything. The more help they get from us to enrich themselves, the more positions they will leave to us.[3]

"Are we really deceiving anyone," asked Li, "if we help some politician—in a district of the Gironde or in England—to win a victory when he has been passed over perhaps a hundred times by his own party because of his incompetence, but whom we can control and who is established in a position to which a communist candidate could never have been appointed?"[4]

Mao Tse-tung pointed out what should be done with men who failed to keep their part of the bargain: They must be attacked with merciless severity and destroyed. This would spread fear, and in the future no one would dare to emulate their behavior. Mao said,

> We must win over the petty bourgeois, just as the Nazis did, so that they will serve our own aims through greed, fear, a sense of inferiority and their desire for revenge and so forth. . . . We must tempt everyone at his own weak point, just as the devil would; help them to acquire all they want; put them under pressure, first with alluring offers and then with threats; compromise them so that they have no way out. . . . The overwhelming majority of our friends and enemies are opportunists, outright opportunists.[5]

A few days later, Ravines discussed his talks to the Chinese with Dimitrov, asking him what qualities a man must have to be asked to cooperate following the criteria of the Yenan way. "Qualities are not important," said Dimitrov. "You must decide who can be useful to the party and who not. That is the sole criterion. Just remember that all our concessions are temporary. Do not forget that we communists are fighting for world revolution. If that revolution triumphs, the steel columns of Communism will march over the corpses of those self-same fellow travellers who are now offering us their protection. There is no alternative. It is an inevitable consequence."[6]

The Development of the Popular Front

After his return from Moscow, Ravines set about his work in Chile under the assumed name of Jorge Montero. Aided by a Czech, Frederick Glaufbaug; a German operating under the name of Manuel Caspon; a Russian named Kasanov who claimed to be Chilean under the name of Casanova; a Venezuelan, Ricardo Martinez; an Italian, Malucci; and a Spaniard, Ravines formed the Popular Front action committee, which was controlled from Moscow, and set about guiding the Chilean Communists in the new direction.

The plan was to overthrow the president, Arturo Alessandri, and to install a bourgeois opposition candidate as president. He, in turn, was to be replaced later by a Communist. The sympathy of intellectuals, such as Pablo Neruda who enjoyed an international audience, must also be gained as a matter of priority. The danger of fascism was emphasized and exaggerated. Lawyers who defended the interests of major corporations in their working days, thundered against imperialism and exploitation in the salons of like-minded people in the evening and also helped to gain credits for the Communist party and its operations. The big banks were only too ready to finance the Soviet International, a tradition which was later taken over by almost all the Western banks and further developed in Germany with great skill.

The principal prop was the Radical party, under whose banner Ravines and his friends wanted to sail to power in line with the wishes of Moscow. In those days the Christian-Democrats in Chile did not exist. That party was formed later when younger members of the Conservative party left the latter. Sons rebelled against their fathers. At that time, the Radical party supported Arturo Alessandri, the president who belonged to the Liberal party, but felt that it was being passed over in favor of the conservatives and liberals when government posts were distributed. Ravines set to work immediately; he organized dinners, held out the attraction of seats as senators and deputies, hinted at the possibility of lucrative positions in state-owned companies, and promised his own "disinterested help" and that of his friends. The common aim of resisting fascism and imperialism must always be borne in mind. The naivete of the bourgeoisie was limitless. Envy of the rich Americans was portrayed as a fight for justice and brought in many fresh recruits. As Malucci put it, "The possibilities which this country holds out for us communists are incredible."

When popular Radical party senator Pedro Leon Ugalde (who had waged a lifelong fight against communism) died, the Communists turned up with great banners at his funeral and paid tribute to him as a "precursor in the fight for the liberty of his enslaved people."

The people of Chile were then stunned when the Communists went on to force through the candidacy of the exiled radical politician Juan Luis Mery for the Left party grouping instead of the Socialist party candidate, Schnake. Mery lost to the government candidate, but Ravines had established himself and his party friends as an important political force whose friendship and assistance were now increasingly sought. As he said, "This is no doubt a great success for the Communist International, its agent the Soviet Union and the great and wise Stalin." The idea of the Popular Front became firmly entrenched within the Radical and Left parties.

Ravines trained his own group to specialize in campaigns of hatred. Cells were organized everywhere to stir up hatred against individuals, institutions, or specific situations. The party became increasingly feared and exercised a kind of blackmailing pressure which was hard to combat. The number of sympathizers was many times greater than that of the party converts and members. "We learned afresh each day to apply the tactic of the Yenan way," Ravines explained. "We exploited neighborly love just as we exploited the cheap ambition of subordinates, the healthy idealism of young people and the hatred of professional rivals. Above all, we were a magnet for every candidate who wanted to be elected to a post of senator, deputy, mayor or council member and who lacked the necessary votes, prestige and specialized knowledge."[7]

This tactic proved particularly successful with the labor unions, since Ravines did not try to install Communist directors or turn the union bosses into Communists. However, they were corrupted, compromised, and used for Communist purposes.

> Each individual case was examined. Services were given, ambitions spurred, greed encouraged and positions offered. Experts in bookkeeping, specialists in labor law and writers were made available to the leaders of the indepen-

dent trade unions. The many minor and more serious problems with which trade unionists are confronted every day were solved by us for them at no cost. Men turned up who began by being mere helpers of the officials, but then gradually became little short of mental directors and took over firm control of the union management. Their leaders were like wax in our hands. Behind each secretary, stenographer and attorney, a cell, committee or directing nucleus operated. Increasingly it was they who dictated the speeches which were given, the notes that were taken and appointments to posts. Thus, independent trade union leaders became our puppets and served us much better than if they had been communists because they were known to the public as persons who did not belong to a party and so their influence was much greater.[8]

Men who resisted were hit with no holds barred. Every conceivable difficulty was placed in their path. Their friends' opinions of them were poisoned; they were isolated and given to understand that they had no future. It was suggested to the workers, for example, that their union leaders had been bought by the capitalists; their confidence in them was then undermined. During a strike, acts of violence were often perpetrated with the result that the trade unionist, who was disliked by the Communists, was arrested by the police or dropped by his own union.

The *Popular Front* newspaper was founded with bank loans and guided to success with the aid of innumerable non-Communists. Ravines laughed at the contributions of these blind idealists. Their efforts created an instrument "whose sole task was to serve the purposes of the Comintern, Russia and our great comrade Stalin."[9] Thus, the Popular Front parties won the Parliamentary elections in 1937, the Communists moved into the Senate, and many of them joined the Chamber of Deputies. In 1938 the first Popular Front candidate, the Radical Pedro Aguirre Zerda, became president of Chile. Another Radical, Gabriel Gonzalez Videla (president of Chile between 1946 and 1952), brought the Communists into the government for the first time in the country's history, but soon recognized the subversive nature of his allies and finally outlawed the Communist party.

In 1939, Ravines broke with the Soviets, partly because he viewed the Stalin/Hitler pact as a betrayal. I met him together with some friends in Buenos Aires in the early 1960s. We asked him about his motives and what had impelled him to do all this. He told us that to begin with he had hungered after social justice. He had believed that the Communist party pointed the way towards that goal. The search for justice had then been replaced by a feeling of power, of being able to control and manipulate men. These factors had guided his entire being until his conscience was aroused and he realized that he had betrayed his own cause by placing the unbridled struggle for power for the few above all other considerations instead of respecting the commitment to the poor and disinherited, which he had championed at the outset. He became an anti-Communist. He also had us understand that he had subsequently recognized that anti-communism was useless and ultimately played into the hands of the Soviets—his relationship was like that of the moon to the sun, or the shadow to the tree, because every "anti" is in some way bound up with its opposite. It remains a reaction which can be manipulated and is no substitute for an independent objective. It is not enough to be against communism—communism must be overcome.

Salvador Allende and Democracy

The tactic of the Yenan Way initiated by Ravines in Chile was resolutely pursued by others and thirty years later brought Salvador Allende to power. He had been politically active for forty years and had tried for twenty to become president. On his fourth attempt, he was elected, a textbook example of a successful Popular Front policy. Earlier, Josef Goebbels, Hitler's chief propagandist, had defined this policy, destroying democracy from within. He explained that the Nazis moved into the Reichstag (Parliament) in order to borrow weapons from the arsenal of democracy, which they could then fight on its own ground. Their purpose was not to participate in the democratic process, but to paralyze the democratic (Weimar) positions with their own support. He laughed at the stupidity of democracy to give them a free hand and pay them salaries to do their subversive work. Like Lenin, he believed that every legal means to advance the revolution is acceptable.

In the Chilean presidential elections of 1970, Allende won 36.2 percent of the votes cast, of which only 13 percent can be attributed to his own Socialist party. The Radical party accounted for 8 percent and the Communists for 15.9 percent, the rest being left-wing splinter groups. The conservative candidate, Jorge Alessandri, won 34.9 percent, and the Christian-Democrat, Radomiro Tomic, 27.8 percent.

As no single candidate had gained an absolute majority, the Chilean Congress now had to elect the president. Allende was elected with the votes of the Christian-Democrats who probably had not read Ravines's book, or failed to take it seriously, just as the Germans and the rest of the world took no account of Hitler's *Mein Kampf.* The Christian-Democrats were simply following an old democratic tradition, according to which the candidate who has gained the most votes is entitled to the presidency. Allende gave them constitutional guarantees, which he had not the slightest intention of respecting. He described this to French Communist Regis Debray as a "tactical necessity."

Radomiro Tomic, the Christian-Democratic presidential candidate and later ambassador to the United States who was defeated by Allende, once described his political attitudes to me. His mental and ideological confusion and that of the Christian-Democrats, as shown in internal discussions of their ideals and aims, still continues today. Their social concepts are based on economic principles, and they are not sure what role Christian thinking should play in this process. They wish to be neither Socialists nor capitalists. They therefore took over the concept of "communitarianism" from Catholic social theory, but very soon transformed it into "Socialist communitarianism" with the vocabulary and action programs which are so familiar to us from the Soviet system. They refer, for instance, to the need to "replace the capitalist structures, which divide Chile, by other," and to "socialize the economy, political and social institutions as well as the educational and cultural sectors." In practice this led to unity of action with Socialists and Communists against the views of the first Christian-Democratic president, Eduardo Frei, who described those forces as the "gravediggers of democracy." The 1989 presidential elections proved that alliance, and the first thing the new government did was raise taxes.

The philosophy introduced and advocated by Tomic, backed by confused liberation theologists within the clergy, still maintains the illusion that such cooperation might be possible. The Christian-Democrats therefore remain a latent risk to democracy in Chile as the more far-sighted Communists may exploit them for their own advantage. It was Tomic who concluded an agreement with Allende in the name of his party friends. He based this decision on the similarity of their declared programs; in so doing, the Christian-Democrats failed to recognize the concealed totalitarian threat, just as many German Democrats did not recognize the true face of Hitler in 1933. Tomic helped Allende to power. But he is a Democrat, and when the Christian-Democrats recognized the course that Allende's policy was taking, they made up for their earlier errors and stood in his way.

For two years, Allende tried to outmaneuver the democratic forces and establish a Soviet-style government. When his attempts failed, he still tried to achieve his ends in breach of the Chilean Constitution and so brought himself into conflict with the legally constituted institutions of Chile. The country declined into economic chaos, the annual rate of inflation exceeded 1,000 percent, and support among the population rapidly dwindled.

The leaders of the Popular Front then decided to definitely abandon the democratic path to power and turned instead to Lenin's route of armed insurrection. Combat groups were formed and armed. The country was full of armed foreigners (some fifteen thousand). Allende's daughter Beatrice, for example, had married a Cuban, who trained and directed the president's own bodyguard. Stores of weapons were set up everywhere, and the president of the Socialist party, Carlos Altamirano, publicly urged the soldiers and non-commissioned officers to disobey their superiors. The book by A. Neuburg entitled *Armed Insurrection* was distributed throughout the country and was called the "Handbook of Crime" by the army.

These events not only exhausted the patience of the armed forces, but also exasperated the Chilean Congress. On 22 August 1973, the House of Representatives declared by a majority vote, with the support of the Christian-Democratic, the National, the Radical-Democratic, and the Left-Radical (now Social-Democratic) parties, that President Allende and his government had placed themselves beyond the bounds of legality and were no longer acting in compliance with the Constitution. Allende himself was officially informed of this decision, as were the commanders of the armed forces, whose task it is to protect the Constitution. The proceedings initiated by the House of Representatives were broadly similar to an American impeachment procedure. The Constitutional Court, Court of Auditors, and Chamber of Attorneys, likewise accused Allende of repeated breaches of the Constitution. The president of the Christian-Democratic party, Patricio Aylwin, who later became president of Chile, compared these developments with events in Czechoslovakia in 1948 which eventually led to the replacement of the democratic order by a Soviet regimen. On 11 September 1973, the armed forces put an end to the totalitarian aspirations of the clique of Soviet quislings. This was not a putsch by power-hungry generals. It was the implementation of the will of Parliament, which had accused the president of breaches of the Constitution and consequently of illegal exercise of power but had no authority to destitute him as can be done, for example, in the United States. This is where the armed forces come in. General Pinochet and the other commanders acted to protect the Constitution. The soldiers upheld the freedom of the Chilean people.

In December 1987, I had a conversation with retired Gen. Rolando Gonzalez, who had been Minister of Mines in Allende's last cabinet. His neighbors used to throw maize into his garden in those days to signify their view that he was a chicken or coward—an indirect challenge to give up his neutrality towards Allende and act. The people wanted the army to act.

In any analysis of these events, the following essential facts should be highlighted:

1. The Soviet takeover through the Popular Front government was conceived in Moscow and blessed by Stalin. Moscow has always controlled and guided the Front since then. This amounts to flagrant intervention in the internal affairs of another country, although the Soviet Union has managed to avoid being perceived as an actor on the scene—as is the case wherever else they are pursuing the same tactic. While Pinochet recognized the real threat against which he defended the country, the rest of the world tried to lecture to him that there is no such threat. It would be interesting to search for evidence now in the KGB files.

2. Chile and the Chilean armed forces have the longest and most deeply rooted democratic tradition in all of Latin America. Unlike the military in Argentina, Brazil, and Bolivia, with whom I worked for many years when I lived there, the Chilean soldiers have always been apolitical. There is the same difference with other Latin American countries. I was able to discover in Peru that many Peruvians judge the situation in Chile in the light of their familiarity with their own generals and reach totally false conclusions. When I visited Chile for the first time in 1958, my uncle, who was the German ambassador at the time, arranged a discussion for me with the commander of the Santiago military region, Gen. Carlos Pollarolo Maggi. I also met Generals Enzio Coda Suziani and Horacio Arce, chief of the army staff. This was shortly before the presidential elections at the end of the six-year term of office of Carlos Ibanez del Campo. At that time, the victory of the Popular Front candidate seemed a serious possibility, but in the end Jorge Allessandri was elected. I asked General Pollarolo what the armed forces would do if a Communist or a candidate supported by the Communists became president. He immediately answered: "As long as he respects the Constitution, we shall serve him." I thought to myself that he was rather naive if he believed that any Communist would respect a constitution, except for tactical purposes.

After Allende had broken the Constitution to which he and the generals had sworn allegiance (forty-six times in all), they no longer wished to serve him and removed him from office. He was repeatedly offered the possibility of leaving the country with an aircraft placed at his disposal. Allende preferred to shoot himself with the rifle which Fidel Castro had given him.

3. Chile has a much longer democratic tradition than Germany. The Chilean generals were and still are Democrats, unlike most German generals of the Hitler era who simply obeyed orders. Hitler put an end to German democracy a few weeks after he was elected chancellor of the Reich, and he did so with the aid of many people who were not Nazis. The German generals and field-marshals allowed him to set up his abyss. They also let themselves be used to assist him in achieving his aims. Allende was defeated by the Democrats and the democratic institutions of Chile. The Chilean generals had more backbone than their German counterparts and put an end to the anti-democratic, totalitarian conspiracy by the force of arms. The Germans were concerned about their reputation, the Chileans about their country.

Allende did not improve the lot of the poor Chileans as he had promised, but rather made it still worse. He set the country back by many years. The economic decline generated by his policies hit the weakest sectors of the population particularly hard; not only did their situation deteriorate, but their prospects for improvement faded into the distant future. Allende was not interested in the poor. He made use of the poor and their desperation. In its 2/88 edition, the German newsmagazine *Der Spiegel* published a photograph of Allende with slum dwellers, with a caption which suggested that he had fought for their rights; that is an incredible assertion. A further picture in the same magazine (4/88 edition) shows the secretary general of the German Christian-Democratic Union (CDU), Heiner Geissler, in the company of slum dwellers in Santiago, with a caption accusing the president of Chile, Pinochet, of indifference to the poor people. That is a lie. Publications of this kind are a manifest manipulation of public opinion by distorting the truth—a practice which has been pursued for years by the gutter-media in the free world. The reality is the exact opposite of what is suggested, as can readily be ascertained from the objective economic data. The same photographs could be used to prove the contrary by simply changing the caption.

Allende met all the requirements defined by Mao Tse-tung, Chu-Te, Dimitrov, and Ravines of what constitutes an obedient Soviet puppet. He was a man who gave the outward appearance of a pleasant or even good person, but in his heart he pursued the satisfaction of his own pleasures. Just one year after he seized power, Santiago came to resemble Moscow, Havana, Luanda, or Managua. Long lines often began to form in the evening in front of every shop; people slept on the streets at night in an attempt to purchase the bare essentials the next morning. Before and after Allende, things were never like that in Chile.

While Allende fed his fellow countrymen with Socialist jargon, they found themselves confronted with increasing terrorism. While the world gave credence to the fairy tale of the "democratic" president, Soviet agents like Ravines took over the reins of the country. Allende was a doctor with a good situation, but he was as ambitious as he was unsuccessful in his political career until the Soviet Popular Front specialists took him under their wing. When he became president, he had already been separated for fourteen years from his wife Hortensia, and almost everyone in the country knew that he had to pay her when protocol required him to appear in the company of the first lady of the country. On the evening before the military coup of 10 September 1973, he was in the company of scantily clad girls in his "Carnaval" country house in El Arrayan on the edge of the Cordillera where he was enjoying these girls, together with an extensive assortment of rich food and alcohol. As a matter of fact, each of his houses was equally well stocked. This occurred while the people whom he governed had to line up in front of shops for hours to get basic goods. In conflict with the tradition of Chilean presidents who always adopted a simple lifestyle, Allende led the dissolute life of a pasha with his mistresses and his harem. After he had been toppled from power, a notary made an inventory and found in his Tomas Moro residence such things as 1,630 ties, 168 suits, and so on. One of Allende's mistresses owned 23 cars. In addition, the notary discovered

pornographic films and gigantic sums in dollars which must be
added to the millions which Allende and his fellow thieves had
already salted away abroad.

Allende ended like Hitler but is still portrayed as the last
Democrat in Chile, who was murdered by the power-hungry
generals led by Pinochet in order to establish a military dictatorship in Chile. The self-righteous Pharisees in Washington, Bonn,
and Paris see the mote in Pinochet's eye, but they are blind to
the beam in their own. They were all part of an international
Popular Front campaign which was controlled from Moscow.

The Chilean Reality of the Eighties and the Western Schoolmasters

Pinochet is a magnet for the hatred and desire for revenge
of all those people whose plans he has thwarted. The art of
defamation and persecution has been perfected since the days of
Ravines. Action, which was then purely local, is pursued today
in the age of mass media with unflagging obstinacy on the
international stage. Just as the Soviets tried in those days to
destroy Ravines morally and financially because of his break
with them, as he told me, a campaign to discredit and destroy
the president of Chile has been in full swing for many years. The
procedure is always the same: Hatred is fueled, lies are spread,
the truth is poisoned, and economic pressure is exerted. Once
again, as in those days, defamation and revenge are simply part
of the increasing endeavor to destroy Chilean democracy and
put the country under totalitarian rule.

The worldwide schizophrenic hysteria over Chile under
Pinochet derives, on the one hand, from the campaign of accu-
sations and hatred controlled by the disinformation department
of the KGB, for which purpose, according to an estimate by the
German Congressman Hans Graf von Huyn, some $200 mil-
lion was spent in the eighties; and, on the other hand, from the
hypocrisy of the rest of the world and especially of the political
leaders who try to force upon Chile their own limited, superficial, and formalistic concept of democracy.

"We cannot be bought. We say yes or no and in that we
differ from the politicians." That is how Pinochet described to

me his own style and that of his government. In fact, because Chile had an uncorrupt government and a clean police force, the country now has the best economic prospects in Latin America. Not only does it service its foreign debt, but between 1986 and 1988 it even reduced that debt from $21 billion to $17 billion. In the last decade, over $80 billion has been shipped out of Mexico. In Chile, on the other hand, not only has there been no capital drain, but investment capital was flowing into the country.

The newsmagazine *Vision* has defined Chile as a unique example on the Latin American scene in terms of the diversification of its economy and its extraordinary exports growth. Pinochet has cut the bureaucracy by half, a decisive measure which no other Latin American president has had the courage to take. At the same time, social expenditure rose from 10.1 percent of Gross Domestic Product in 1980 to 15.1 percent in 1985. In a report entitled "Poverty in Latin America" published by the World Bank in September 1986, we read: "The Chilean example is particularly interesting in that it reflects a successful attempt to direct the government's social expenditure towards the poorest sections of the population. . . . Chile's control of social expenditure is unique in the region." The World Bank, the International Monetary Fund, and the Inter-American Development Bank all maintain that Chile has mastered the crisis better than any other country. While social housing construction has reached an unprecedented scale, assets are also being spread broadly across the population. In 1987, some 350,000 Chileans became new shareholders. In 1987, the inflation rate was extraordinarily low for Latin America at 16 percent; it fell below 12 percent in 1988. In 1988, real Gross National Product rose by over 6 percent; 300,000 new jobs were created; and real incomes grew by 6.5 percent.

The description of Pinochet as a dictator and Allende as a Democrat is a perverse distortion of reality. In the 1970 presidential elections, Allende polled some 20 percent of the non-Communist votes—in fact, the votes of his own Socialist party should really be counted in the Communist camp. The overwhelming majority of Chileans breathed again when his regime came to an end. The generals took over a bankrupt country. Throughout his term of office, Pinochet has always had more Democratic supporters than Allende had during his years as president.

In the referendum in 1989, he obtained 45 percent—a much higher percentage than the governing Christian-Democratic party in Germany wins. It is true that he lost, and as a Democrat he stepped aside, but it wasn't the resounding rejection of the Chilean people that Western media reported.

There was naturally always opposition, especially from politicians who did not hold power. There has also always been opposition in the press, which was unrestrained in its criticism of the regime. Significantly, there were an independent judiciary and an independent court of auditors, whose decisions were respected by the government while Allende disregarded them. I personally consider Chile to be a country in which the rule of law has always been respected; that is certainly not the case in Mexico. In Chile there is no need to pay judges (Pinochet or no Pinochet) to obtain a fair verdict; I am merely exposed to their possible errors. In Mexico, even court secretaries and messengers want to see the color of my money before they take any action, as do most of the judges.

In Panama at the time of Noriega, a taxi driver described his country's government to me as a dictatorship dressed up as a democracy. By his definition, the substance of the regime was not democratic although there was a parliament with elected representatives of the people. In Chile, on the other hand, the substance was democratic, although the external form did not correspond to the ideas of Western fanatics of democracy. But even the form was not that of a dictatorship. The underlying motives of the generals were the decisive factor, and I see them as identical with those of the military leaders with whom I met thirty years earlier; they wish to serve their country in faithful obedience to the Constitution. One could count on the fingers of one hand the Latin American leaders of whom the same could be said. "Our government is acting to safeguard the human rights of all the 11 million Chileans," was the comment of one Chilean outraged by the continuing verbal attacks on his country.

It is all the more reprehensible when foreigners travel to Chile in order to give their hosts lectures about democracy and human rights. The most flagrant examples are those of the German minister of labor, Norbert Blum, and secretary general of the Christian-Democratic Union, Heiner Geissler. Blum came partly to offer asylum in the Federal Republic to fourteen "Chileans who had been sentenced to death." In Germany the foreign minister, Hans-Dietrich Genscher, a member of the Liberal Coalition party, had asked for these persons to be granted asylum. The Social-Democrats had also taken up the cause of these "innocent victims," and a substantial section of the German press contained almost daily attacks on the injustice and tortures to which these Chileans were purportedly exposed in the prisons of the dictator Pinochet.

In fact, these fourteen included terrorists in the Al Fatah style, convicted murderers, and bank robbers who had not only shot two officers, but also a parking lot attendant and a bank employee during a bank robbery. I doubt whether they were tortured in prison, which is where they belong. It is shameful that the German government and public opinion should be seriously negotiating asylum for criminals. Even more shameful is the spectacle of these two Christian-Democrats in Chile, where they undermined German prestige. Genscher, who quite obviously did not listen to his own ambassador in Chile, was interested in turning Chilean human rights problems to his own domestic political advantage and sought to increase his popularity with the United Nations; this revealed a terrifying lack of principle in German foreign policy.

Blum came to Chile resolved to outdo his coalition partner Genscher and hang the same subject onto his own political banner. Apparently he took a tape recorder with him in his pocket to tape the conversation he had with Pinochet; on his return he handed the tapes over to the newsmagazine *Der Spiegel*. What he said in Chile was actually intended for his German voters since he could not have been interested in justice for the

Chileans themselves. He also knows nothing about the Chilean legal system. Did he realize what he was saying when he told journalists at that time that there were no Communists in Germany? I don't think he did because Germany was in fact full of Communists who then controlled a large sector of the country. Some of them advanced after reunification to the German Parliament in Bonn.

Blum was infringing the spirit and letter of Germany's own Constitution, which has always taken Germany as one nation. Its preamble speaks of a "transitional period" until the whole German people will be able to live in a united and free Germany on the basis of free self-determination. Article 23 of the Constitution reads: "This law shall take effect in other parts of Germany once they become members (of the Federal Republic)." In its ruling of July 1973, the Federal German Constitutional Court confirmed this disposition. "Unity and justice and freedom for the German fatherland"—anybody who sang our national anthem without having a personal commitment to attain it for all Germans was a hypocrite. Blum evidently believed that our German countrymen (and the territory beyond the barbed wire in which they lived) no longer belonged to our country. He had written them off. It is not to the merit of politicians like Blum that the fence came down later on (although Blum immediately transformed himself into a champion of unification).

The Chilean leaders were faithful to their Constitution. They must have considered the lecturing on democracy and human rights by a member of the German government who fails to respect his own Constitution as a macabre gesture, especially when that same government concurrently welcomed into Bonn the Soviet quisling, builder of the wall, issuer of orders to shoot, and spurner of human rights—Erich Honecker—with a guard of honor from the Bundeswehr who presented arms to him. The Central Investigating Bureau of the Federal German States, which recorded illegal acts of violence on the territory of the Communist state, had at that time registered 2,438 cases of violence against prisoners since 1961. Being in power, Honecker was appeased by the West German government hypocrites. Only after the wall had come down and Honnecker appeared to be stripped of power was he called a criminal and were charges filed for criminal acts that for all those years were clear to everyone. The West German government therefore was an accomplice in having kept him in power for so long. But this does not prevent them from attacking the Chilean government. German justice therefore seems to amount to the acceptance of injustice at home while attacking others, but certainly not everywhere—only in those countries where political capital can be made.

These German politicians seemed to be totally unaware of the schizophrenic nature of their actions. Geissler, for example, conducted his electoral campaign from Chilean soil, in the sure expectation that any attack on Pinochet would be repaid in electoral votes and cash back home. His conduct and statements in Chile were far removed from reality. I do not believe that it is for him (or any other foreign politician) to intervene in the election campaign of another country as massively as he did when he called upon the Chileans to vote "no" in the referendum and, in full public view, gave further advice to boycott the political and economic process in his host country. Even if the government of that country gave him the liberty to attack it on its own territory instead of expelling him, this irresponsible, tactless, schoolmasterly conduct by a Christian-Democrat is hard to swallow, and has nothing whatever to do with Christianity. I was as ashamed at the German lack of sensitivity as in the immediate postwar years when I faced the Chileans in Santiago.

Geissler, concerned only with his own personality and ideas, was as neglectful as Blum of the fact that the conceptual structures which in his linguistic area and territory are not called into question by his mentally lazy accomplices of prosperity, and was scarcely convincing abroad. He presented himself in Chile as the representative of the authentic free market economy and denied Chile the right to speak of itself in the same breath as our own exemplary model "since the social market economy does not mean wealth for the few and poverty for the many," as Geissler said with an accusing finger.

It verges on the comical when Geissler quotes the German trade union state as the model of a free market economy. Instead of giving free rein to the market forces, as Ludwig Erhard imagined, artificial barriers have been created in Germany, such as shop opening hours which are prejudicial both to economic growth and to the creation of jobs, making shopping more difficult, particularly for families. Every shop closes at 6:30 P.M. and there is no weekend shopping.

In Latin America we usually do our family shopping on Saturday afternoon and Sunday because we do not have the time on weekdays, although the shopping centers stay open until 8 p.m. When, in light of this, workers in Germany strike to obtain a thirty-five-hour work week, one is left with the impression that the Germans live in an unreal world and have no genuine awareness of needs in the developing countries. Instead of striking for a shorter work week, they might, for example, work one hour more each day and pay the corresponding wage into a fund for the benefit of the developing countries. There could also be no objection to a few hours overtime for that same purpose.

Over DM 50 billion are paid out in tax money each year for subsidies in the Federal Republic which distort competition; it is true that they preserve a few jobs in Germany, but they are harmful to Germany's long-term economic competitiveness and also curtail the developing countries' share of the world market. The true situation is readily illustrated by the example of sugar, which is not an individual case but can be taken as representative of many other commodities.

Sugar is the third most important source of hard currency for Latin America. Two and a half million people are employed in this sector. German farmers are paid about eighty-eight dollars for one hundred kilos of sugar (that is 0.72 cts. per pound), four to five times more than the world market price at which Latin American growers are forced to sell their sugar. The difference between the world market price and the price paid to the German farmers is compensated by the German government and the European Community to the tune of billions, as part of this absurd market-distorting policy. In this way, Latin American growers are deprived of their market and forced to accept a completely inadequate price. Another absurd and distorting feature of the German policy of subsidies is the fact that hundreds of millions of deutsche marks in taxpayers' money are used for the destruction of surplus food products. Geissler's German sugar-growing farmers become richer, while Latin American sugar-growing peasants become impoverished.

The economic crisis in the Dominican Republic can be largely traced back to this fact: the absence of a market and a price for its main export commodity (sugar) and excessively low revenue. Early in 1988, Pres. Joaquin Balaguer was forced to pay a begging visit to Washington to seek U.S. financial aid for his country; aid was promised him. However, aid is not a long-term solution and cannot replace structural clean-up of our corrupted market economy. In 1985, the U.S. Congress voted by 234 to 142 against the wishes of the Reagan government, and to the detriment of U.S. consumers and Latin American countries, an annual subsidy of $3 billion to support the sugar prices of national growers. As one result, the manufacturers of sugar substitutes were also able to obtain excessively high prices, while Latin American exports fell dramatically. Some American companies have earned spectacular profits. They became richer and the Latin Americans poorer. In another vote in 1990 the subsidy was upheld.

Before the vote in 1985, substantial electoral campaign subsidies were paid by the sugar lobby to many congressmen. One hundred percent of those who received more than five thousand dollars voted in favor of the subsidy; contributions of between twenty-five hundred dollars and five thousand dollars resulted in 97 percent support, while payments of one thousand dollars to twenty-five hundred dollars elicited 67 percent votes in favor of the subsidy. Instead of giving his inadmissible lecture to the Chileans, Geissler (the self-proclaimed representative of the free market economy), should have pointed his finger at the atrocious selfishness of the industrial nations. He clearly does not have the courage to do so since it might cost him votes. But the courageous statesman ran no risk of that kind when he attacked Pinochet.

In Chile, Geissler and Blum clearly showed how crude our political customs have become when politicians no longer seek truth and justice but instead use every possible political weapon, including the deliberate distortion of truth, character assassination and deformation of other countries, provided that this brings personal and political party benefits. "Do not bear false witness against your neighbor" is a Commandment which may perhaps not be understood by godless journalists; however, it should surely be heeded by Christian politicians. But they have already thrown it overboard and fail to realize that fact any longer. Thus the corruption of the political opportunism of the blind and deaf prospers. In my opinion, the military leaders of Chile of that time had more character than their "democratic" critics around the world.

In April 1991, one year after becoming president of Chile, Patricio Alwyn made a trip through Europe. In each capital he visited, he made it a point to distance himself from General Pinochet, implying that "the dictator is gone and I, the democrat, have taken over." I am not very impressed with Alwyn's behavior, because I believe that Alwyn had doubtful motives: appease the manipulated world opinion and be liked by the leaders. There was not one word of recognition of the fact that he had inherited the finest economy in Latin America, contrary to Pinochet, who had to begin with a country in ruins. Since 1984, Gross National Product has grown by an average of 6.5 percent; in 1992 the growth rate even reached 10 percent. Most people believe about Chile and Pinochet what they have been fed by the media for so many years. Most government leaders are incapable of thinking outside prefabricated patterns and are too busy and lazy to think for themselves on the basis of objective facts. Once during lunch at the Hyatt Hotel in Denver, I was attacked in the rudest way by a Norwegian, who I thought was my friend. Without any consideration for the other people having their lunch, he shouted at me, denouncing my "disgraceful" positive comments on Pinochet in my book. He had neither read my book, nor had he ever been in Latin America or Chile. Somebody had mentioned to him something I had written and the rest of his opinions probably came from whatever newspaper he had read. But that is the reality of the so-called world opinion, millions of people think precisely the same as he without knowing anything. They know only what is presented to them by the Allende fellow travellers in the media who detest a conservative patriot like Pinochet. Politicians, as usual, take the easy road and adjust themselves to this reality for their own political advantage, even if they know better.

One does not need to endorse all of Pinochet's actions or have the same opinions; and I am not saying that there may not have been violations of human rights during his government. I am quite certain, though, that the violation of fundamental rights is much more substantial in Mexico or even in the abortion-infested United States and Germany, than it was in Chile. I have found the general to be a warm-hearted and likable human being. When I had lunch with him in his headquarters with a number of his top generals and members of his last cabinet, he did not impose himself at all and we had a very lively discussion on world affairs. Everybody offered his opinions without any attempt to please the boss, who listened attentively to what everybody had to say. That is not the way dictators, who I have studied, behave. Yeltsin says that Gorbachev likes to listen only to himself and not to others and speaks for hours. I prefer Augusto Pinochet to the numerous slick politicians I have met and consider him an outstanding and courageous Latin American statesman.

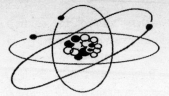

The Chinese Illusion

"What do you think of the situation?," I asked my neighbor on the Lufthansa flight to Beijing early in July 1989; he was a Spaniard, an official of the United Nations returning to China after several weeks in Europe. The Spanish Catholic quoted the words of a German philosopher, whose name I have forgotten: "Order takes precedence over justice. The Chinese government had no option other than to put down the student movement— after all, it could not simply stand idly by and allow its authority to be flouted." Thus he spoke out in favor of the government of a country which is a permanent member of the Security Council of the United Nations, an organization committed by its statutes to the cause of human rights. "After all, the situation will settle down again."

But it will not settle down for the cyclist who was pursued by a tank on Tiananmen Square, run over and deliberately flattened, one of the untold millions of paving stones on the path to socialism. Hundreds and even thousands of civilians were slaughtered with the same brutality on the nights of 3-4 June 1989. Early in the morning, before first light, the corpses were heaped together, soaked in gasoline and burned; the remains were shovelled onto trucks and driven away as another eyewitness, who had been able to observe events from the window of his apartment in an access road to the Square, reported. I spoke with a girl student and was told that two of her comrades had been shot. Her roommate was in prison.

I was able to see the expressionless faces of the soldiers everywhere; they stood guard under umbrellas on every bridge or marched through the streets of Beijing in small platoons. When I expressed astonishment to my taxi driver and a tourist guide at the fact that soldiers with automatic weapons could be seen standing under umbrellas, I had the impression that my inter- locutors were frightened by my words which they might perhaps have taken as a dangerous criticism. I quickly added that in the days when I was a soldier, nobody offered me an umbrella. Loud laughter lightened the atmosphere and they went on to express their concern at the possible future course of events.

When I left the Heavenly Temple, I was suddenly sur- rounded by a group of soldiers. One put his arm through mine and another took a photograph. I suppose that it must have been published in some newspaper to show me as a foreigner sympathetic to the cause. But I am not sympathetic at all. The astonishment and horror of the Western world at the brutality of the government's intervention seems naive to me. Already in Tibet, the Chinese Communist murder state had killed one- quarter of the population, 1.2 million Tibetans. In those days, there were no television cameras. As a reward for its acts, Red China was admitted to the United Nations by the opportunists in Western government clothing. Given its own expertise in matters of internal security, it must surely meet all the necessary requirements for the Security Council.

On this occasion, the massacre was directed solely at fellow countrymen who are as fed up with their regime as were the Poles, the Russians, and the Germans, to say nothing of the Tibetans. The West had obviously also forgotten the millions of corpses which had already fallen victims in earlier days to the Communist version of respect for human rights in China. One and a half million Chinese demonstrated in June 1989 in Beijing; they were certainly not all students. There were also journalists and delegations from all parts of the country, including almost all the government services. Countless participants in the dem- onstrations disappeared immediately after the repression to avoid the reign of terror, and many ministries had to work with a reduced staff, as I was told.

The movement in favor of democracy was not trying to overthrow the government, but only demanding more personal freedom within the Communist system: Freedom of the press and freedom to organize their own lives. The Chinese too want to be able to live normal lives. But they are prevented from doing so by a body of functionaries who regulate every hour of their existence. For example, every Chinese subject in Beijing belongs to a unit which organizes his working life. But he himself cannot choose or influence that unit or the nature of his professional activity. Somebody decides for him; it is as though the mayor of Pocatello, Idaho (where my son studies), were to decide that Stefan will be a hairdresser and he would have to adopt that career without the possibility for him or me to do anything about it. The Chinese require permits for everything, even to marry and have children (or rather one child, since couples are only allowed one), unless they are senior officials or able to bribe such a dignitary. These protest demonstrations were therefore directed primarily against the abuse of power by officials who siphon off the cream for themselves and their families, and place endless difficulties in the way of their dependent subjects—a practice which, as we have seen elsewhere in this book, is not confined to China. The bloody unrest in India in the summer of 1989 was caused by the same phenomenon.

On the other hand, even after the massacre, Beijing has a much more human face than Moscow. There are restaurants, markets, countless shops, and millions of cyclists who are apparently all color blind because they take no notice of traffic lights. They ride through crossroads when the lights are red, perhaps paying just a little more attention to the traffic. In brief, individual life still exists. During a short visit to the province of Canton, that impression was later confirmed by the existence of private enterprise in agriculture. I saw, for example, countless duck farms on which, curiously enough, white ducks were bred, although I had been told that Beijing ducks are large white birds while their Cantonese counterparts are brown and small. I didn't have enough time to sample them.

However, the government is trying to destroy this impression of individuality and bring Beijing into line with the monotorious face of Moscow. Impersonal concrete blocks are sprouting up everywhere and the city is losing its Chinese and oriental flavor which still can be noticed in the back streets.

The propaganda machinery of the lie was already in full swing on my arrival and everybody was involved in the lies. In the English-language *Beijing Daily*, I was able to follow the party line which I then found reflected in a similar vein by Henry Kissinger and others in the West, like the U. N. official on my flight to Beijing. There was no alternative but to repress this rebellion which had been fomented by a small minority of counter-revolutionaries to topple the progressive Socialist order. Very few people had been killed. The ringleaders would be punished but the great mass of those whom they had led astray—people who did not recognize the truth—would be forgiven, and the new open economic policy of the country and its reorientation would naturally continue. Deng Xiao-ping was years ahead of Gorbachev; the clever Chinese had recognized much earlier than the Russians that they could not progress economically with their rigidly controlled state economy. I do not know whether the Chinese government is just as bankrupt as its Soviet sister was, but the trend is surely the same.

The Soviet budget deficit which was naturally not described as such to Western creditors by Gorbachev's liars, already accounted for 30 percent of USSR state revenue in 1985. According to a calculation by Judy Shelton, that shortfall, measured in terms of equivalent revenue, would correspond to twice the already very high budget deficit of the United States in 1987. In compensation, the Soviet government printed paper money and tried at the same time to motivate workers by wage increases, naturally without success. Since productivity had been declining for fifteen years and more money was being pumped into the economy with no corresponding increase in the supply of goods, the situation resulted in the dissolution of the Soviet Union. It was like Germany in the postwar years when citizens could not buy anything with their plentiful paper money. But a monetary and economic reform on the lines of the German 1948 reform which sparked the German economic miracle, was inconceivable in the Soviet Empire; firstly, because neither Gorbachev nor anyone in his hierarchy intended to cut the bureaucratic state apparatus—an essential prerequisite; and secondly, because Soviet citizens, after seventy years of bureaucratic rule, are no longer capable of independent work and do not have the necessary technology. So the Soviet Union began to break up. Gorbachev's half-hearted and superficial reforms only increased discontent and repulsion of the regime.

As in the Soviet Union, the corrective economic measures taken in China have been misunderstood in the West as a move towards democracy, and the competition to gain market shares has begun under the pretext of assisting the process of democratization. Neither Deng nor the dismissed general secretary, Zhao Ziang, nor any of the party leaders, ever intended to question the domination of the Communist party and grant political freedom. The tightrope walk between economic reforms, with corresponding economic progress on the one hand and political control on the other, was successful for many years. The West pumped billions into China. But then the spirits which the Chinese leadership had summoned up acquired a life of their own and ran out of control, as happened to Gorbachev. Economic liberties, which allowed the individual to organize himself according to his own criteria and better the life of his family, led to demands of greater political freedom. The authorities struck back, after disagreeing for weeks over the kind of action to take. The leaders agreed on the need to put an end to the people's movement, but they could not agree how. The murderous brutality of the repression then was not an excess, but a display of pure Leninism, controlled terror designed to generate fear.

Fear is a prerequisite for Communist rule and the students, together with an increasing number of Chinese, had begun to lose the fear as everybody could see from the uninhibited faces of the demonstrating students on Western television. The events on Tiananmen Square on the nights of 3-4 June were not isolated; for a moment the regime was simply showing its true face which nobody in the West had been prepared to recognize for some time. The brutality was also not an expression of stubborn old age but merely a reflection of the resolve of all the participants to preserve power. The wave of arrests, public humiliations, and executions of the ringleaders are all part of a cold-blooded process designed to terrorize and intimidate the Chinese people.

On my visit to Beijing in July 1989, I was able to observe that the process had been largely, but not completely, successful. Here too the Chinese government is walking a tightrope between the terror, which from its point of view, is essential and the desire to woo the West and Japan whose money and technology are naturally needed to strengthen China's own position of power. The Chinese will have to live with terror for a long time to come. Caught up in his life of hedonism, Western man will soon have forgotten these events.

American policy towards China is based on an incorrect analysis. The American ambassador to Beijing, James Lilley, demonstrated his inability to recognize the true substance in an NBC interview on 10 June 1989 when he said: "The events on Tiananmen Square are an aberration. We hope that everything will return to normal, and that China will become a prosperous, and friendly nation." Pres. George Bush, speaking from the White House, said that relations with the Chinese people and their government are too important to be endangered by drastic measures. He added categorically: "We cannot create a new world." I differ and say we must. Bush, apart from applying different standards in the case of Peru, Panama, and Haiti with less cause, is perpetuating the same error as his predecessors a few decades before, who equated subjugated people with their totalitarian rulers. Lilley fails to recognize the basic principle of any Communist government, which is to demand subservience; this is not changed by corrective economic measures. The *China Daily* made this point in its lead article on 28 June 1989: "Capitalism today is no longer the same as in those days. We can of course take over some aspects for the benefit of socialism which will naturally carry victory in the end." And so the Chinese government was able at the beginning of 1991 to have leading dissidents like Chen Xiaoping put up for trial without having to fear Western reprisals. The rest of the world was occupied with its indignation of Saddam Hussein, and America wanted the Chinese help to fight him. Hundreds of dissidents continue in prisons. Prime and foreign ministers begin again to arrive in Beijing and, after paying lipservice to their hypocritical Human Rights concept, do business as usual. Deng had predicted that in 1989: "Foreigners will again knock at our door, once we have stabilized the political situation and got the economy working."

Just as the forces seeking freedom in China acquired a momentum of their own which ran counter to the wishes of the rulers, so the economic and financial investments by Western countries have also developed their own momentum which no government can resist any longer. Since Western politicians merely pay lip service to ethical principles but largely fail to practice them, they will now have to try to save the investments and jobs of their electors through projects such as the well-advanced engineering work by Siemens and AEG on the Shangai subway system. I therefore consider the imposition of sanctions as no more than window-dressing by the superficial, hypocritical, and aimless West, which must constantly confirm its own morality to itself. In the early days after the massacre, the process of "exceptions" began and pressure towards "business as usual" got well underway, exactly as was the case after Afghanistan, Prague, or Budapest. Six months later, that principle was well established again. American government subsidies for wheat exports to China continue.

Deng, like Gorbachev, can always count on helpers such as Kissinger who make developments palatable to the business-hungry West through their sage remarks. In his article "America Cannot Do Without China," published in Germany's *Welt am Sonntag* on 30 July 1989, this strategist of Western decline and exponent of Western moral double standards clearly defined the basis on which the policy of appeasement is nourished: On lies. "What has happened in Beijing must not be seen solely from the angle of good and evil," Kissinger tells us and goes on to push that principle aside immediately by developing a number of arguments, all designed to make the totalitarian Chinese rulers acceptable. Kissinger's statement in fact means that application of the principle of good or evil in politics is incompatible with the interests of the United States and that the Bush government can only maintain its position in Asia by disregarding truth.

The cynicism of this Nobel Peace Prize winner is equally repulsive when he explains that, in the case of a small country like South Africa, a "marginal player on the international scene," it is admissible to interfere in the internal affairs of another country by imposing sanctions "but it would be very stupid to apply the same principle of intervention to such a large and powerful country as China." "Does the United States want to take the responsibility for actually toppling the Chinese government?" he asks and immediately gives a negative answer to his own question. So he wants to support that government. On the other hand, in the case of South Africa, the declared aim of the strategist of sanctions always was to topple the Boer regime.

However, the consequence of political action in both cases is a strengthening of the totalitarian, anti-democratic forces and a weakening of the democratic camp. Since Kissinger fails to recognize the link between universal morality and successful politics, he is weakening America and the free world. The question is not whether to apply sanctions, make investments, write off or accommodate China—no, the basic issue is that of truth and lies. Only by respecting the principle of equal justice for all, including ourselves (i.e., a rejection of the double morality of Kissinger), is it possible to establish a policy which meets the true needs of men in all countries, including one's own.

China is as repressive as any totalitarian state. Valerie Strauss and Daniel Southerland reported in a two-part series in the *Washington Post* carried in a syndicated article by Steven Chapman in the *Gazette Telegraph* on 8 August 1995, that the death toll under Mao was "at least 40 million and perhaps 80 million or more." "Only" 12 million people were killed in Hitler's concentration camps.

In June 1995 Amnesty International released a report stating that torture, forced labor, and detention without trial underpin worsening political repression in China. Already in February 1994, the U.S.-based human rights group Asia Watch had pointed out that 1993 was the worst year for political arrests and trials since the crackdown on the democracy movement in 1989. Political repression is increasing, the report said, and not decreasing as some U.S. officials have said. In May 1994, the same group, together with another group, Human Right in China, listed hundreds of newly detained dissidents, saying that the known detainees are just the "tip of the iceberg." The report also said that China is selling prison-made goods in the United States, contrary to earlier promises to stop the practice. Chinese dissident and naturalized American citizen, Harry Wu, had exposed in two books, *Lao-gai—the Chinese Gulag* and *Bitter Winds— memories of my years in China's Gulag,* how the cruel prison camp system works. Together with BBC reporter Sue Lloyd-Robert, he produced a video tape showing the executions of prisoners whose organs were being removed right after the execution and sold at Western black market prices by the Chinese government for hard cash. This video was shown to the Senate Committee on Foreign Relations.

The U.N. Fourth World Conference on Women in Beijing in September 1995, a frontal attack on the moral foundations of Western civilization, cannot be seen different than as an endorsement of the Red Chinese inhumanities by all those governments represented there. Whatever reasons given or speeches made on human rights, their presence beefs up an immoral government. They share the responsibility for those atrocities as much as we German bystanders, who did not speak up and took the consequences; we were co-responsible for the atrocities of Hitler.

In the U.N. World Conference of Human Rights in Vienna in June 1993, China succeeded in excluding the Dalai Lama of Tibet from the official program of the conference. China, Cuba, Syria, and Yeomen were elected vice-chairmen of the conference, an insult to freedom-loving people and a demonstration of the spineless opportunism of Western governments, selling us down the drain.

The Chinese government has killed 1.2 million Tibetans, a third of the population. The intent of that government "is to suppress (Tibetans) completely and in the meantime to increase the Chinese population so that in a few years' time, the Tibetans become insignificant in their own land," said the Dalai Lama in an interview published in the *Los Angeles Times* on 13 May 1995.

Western businesses committed $110.85 billion to projects in China during 1993, according to a report in the *Wall Street Journal* on 2 February 1994. In November 1993, Chancellor Helmuth Kohl of Germany travelled with part of his cabinet and one hundred top industrialists to Beijing, and German industry has been booking orders in the billions while at the same time at home condemning the evils of totalitarian Germany under Hitler. "Never again," they say, but their deeds betray their pious words. Money in the form of Chinese orders is more important than principle. When the secretary general of the Chinese Communist party and head of state, Jiang Zemin, visited Bonn in July 1995 to sign multibillion dollar investment deals, German Foreign Minister Klaus Kinkel, with the applause of the German press, stressed China's importance for peace and stability. I find this dishonest opportunism of the German leadership repulsive. Jiang Zemin holds precisely the same positions and philosophy as Erich Honecker of former East Germany—who was declared to be a criminal after he was out of power, but not before. Of course, Jiang Chemin holds the key to a huge market—that makes everything different. Honecker and Jiang Zemin share the same inhumanity and murderous state terror with Adolf Hitler. Still, money greedy Western politicians and businessmen find beautiful words to disguise what is nothing else but collaboration with and appeasement of evil for a profit. And that is what brought Germany down in those twelve Hitler years—not the crimes of the Nazis and not the armies of the victors, but the cowardliness and appeasement of those who should have stood up. And of course the U.S. cannot allow herself to be left behind: While Haiti gets an economic blockade, China gets most-favored-nation-trade status.

According to U.S. intelligence sources, thousands of Soviet scientists and technicians have found new employment in China for research, development, and production of advanced weapons. According to *U.S. News and World Report*, these include a new generation of mobile, solid fuel intercontinental missiles capable of reaching Washington and an up-to-date version of the Soviets' MIG series of tactical aircraft.

In July 1989, there was only one subject of conversation in Hong Kong and Macao: How to escape from Red Chinese rule when the British and Portuguese withdraw at the end of the century. The area of Hong Kong consists of approximately one thousand square miles. The colony is divided into the island of Hong Kong with the capital of the Crown Colony, Victoria; the peninsula Kaulun with the city of the same name; the Hinterland of the peninsula; the so-called New Territories; and finally 236 islands which in their majority are uninhabited. In 1898, China leased to Britain the New Territories and some islands, except Hong Kong and Kaulun—those were direct property of the Crown. China has no legal right to them, which according to international law could be forced through against the will of a population with democratic rights. The population concerned here consists of various millions of people.

While politicians talk and negotiate, individuals view their future with fatalism and look for ways of escape. The British Foreign Minister Geofrey Howe was booed and the Crown prince and his wife given to understand that their planned visit in the autumn of 1989 was undesirable. Hong Kong feels betrayed by Great Britain. All the residents who hold foreign passports are seen as privileged people who are envied and who everyone would like to emulate. Drawing on the experience of centuries of colonial policy, the British government had, as a precaution, downgraded the British passports of 3.25 million Hong Kong Chinese into second-class documents, so that although they look like British passports, they are not that at all. Without a visa, they will neither allow the holder to visit London nor to live in England when the Red Chinese arrive, as the Anglican Christian Howe told the Hong Kong population during his visit in the summer of 1989. He is not affected by the problem created by Margaret Thatcher's capable government for Hong Kong residents. But after 1992, anyone who holds a passport of one member state of the European Community, is able to move and settle freely within that community. The other European governments may decide whether they intend to take part in this English racist discrimination against the Chinese, which the London government claims does not actually amount to that.

The essence of the imperialistic colonial policy includes the process of disposing of individuals as the colonial power thinks fit because they are considered too stupid or have been militarily defeated. Nobody has consulted the people of Hong Kong. The "principle" subscribed to by Margaret Thatcher in the Falkland Islands conflict, namely the will of the people to maintain the British flag there, is therefore not a principle but an argument to veil national self-seeking, since the people of the Falklands are English. But the Hong Kong Chinese are not white and are to be handed over against their will by their unimaginative overlords to the Communist criminals. The same fate threatens 6.5 million people in Hong Kong and Macao, where the Portuguese are emulating the English practice and are threatened with the same fate.

There is of course always a formal justification to veil immoral behavior. In this instance, it is the Anglo-Chinese lease treaty which was concluded for a hundred years and expires in 1997 (1999 in Macao). The proprietor must therefore be given back his property and Britain is only respecting its treaty commitment. No mention is made of the fact that this treaty is confined to the New Territories. But the British authorities declare that the island and Kaulum are not viable on their own and so they are thrown also into the jaws of the totalitarians. This in turn raises the question as to whether the Communist government is legally constituted, and therefore the legal heir to the original signatory.

Here again, the West, with its political opportunism, has turned an unlawful government into an equal partner. No Communist government has any legal foundation since its origin lies neither in the will of the people nor in any morally founded principle of law, but purely and simply in violence.

The only difference is that in some instances this violence is more apparent than in others. The West therefore legalizes a violence which is ultimately seeking its own destruction and accepts the brazen endeavor of a Communist government to present itself as a state like any other at face value. But Communist states are not like any other. While the objective in Panama, for example, was to bring the actions of the ruling clique into conformity with the existing legal order, achievable only through a change of individuals, something more fundamental is at stake in a Communist state: The elimination of a state structure developed on the basis of injustice and lies, which conflicts with human dignity and freedom and cannot be democratized, even if its leaders change. Just as the South African government threw a spinner in the works of the democratic forces in Namibia, instead of strengthening them, and so paved the way for a totalitarian Sam Nujoma to rise to power, so the English in Hong Kong have kept the political awareness of the population on the back burner and signed the handover of the territory to China before a proper democratic structure had been established—a scandalous slave trading in the twentieth century.

The Sino-British Agreement states that Hong Kong will be allowed to maintain its capitalist system for fifty years after 1997. After the repression of the democratic movement in China, the Chinese party leader, Jiang Ze-min, declared that the principle of "one land, two systems" on which the agreement is based, remains valid. However, that conceptual structure is an illusion, for us at least, as it is rooted not in reality but in Western materialistic thinking based on economic criteria.

The reality is that there is a confrontation of two fundamentally different value systems. On the one side is the rejection of God with the consequence of despising and disregarding man, whose value is determined by his function in society. The organized expression of this concept on the political level is the totalitarian Communist—and also the Nazi state; on the economic level it is the Socialist state-controlled economy. On the other side is the belief that man is made to the image of God and therefore has an intrinsic value independent of his function. The political expression of this concept is democracy, in which not only everybody can participate in electing his government, but where the right of minorities and of the weak are being protected. On the economic level this concept led to the free market economy. On one side everything is relative, and, at least on the level of the political leadership, lying, cheating, and murdering is permitted to further one's goals. The basis of the other side consists of absolute moral standards. The political and economic orders on both sides are but the consequences of the value system adhered to and established before.

When we in the West now speak of the victory of the free market economy (capitalism), over the centrally controlled economy (socialism), we demonstrate that we do not understand the substance of the developments. The reason for this can be found in our attitudes, that we are abandoning with growing speed our own value system and adopting the relativity of the other side. And that fact shatters the thesis that freedom and democracy are victoriously advancing. I believe that the contrary is the case. We are busy to destroy the very foundations on which freedom and democracy grew.

China, like the Soviet Union, now wishes to benefit from the economic fruits of the original Western values without at the same time giving up its own godless value system. That is of course quite impossible. But until the confused West realizes it, billions of dollars will have been misguidedly invested.

The fact that the transfer of Hong Kong to Chinese rule is not in the first place a matter of economic systems but a question of power, has been made clear by a leading Beijing functionary in Hong Kong, Xu Jia-tun, director of the Xinhua News Agency. He stated in early July 1989 that those parties which sought to exploit Hong Kong as a base for subversion of the Socialist order in China would be severely repressed. Now, if the "propagation and active support for the spread of bourgeois liberalism" is a punishable offense in China which may even result in execution, the inhabitants of Hong Kong will soon be incorporated into this "legal system." A foretaste of what awaits them was obtained by the people of Hong Kong when the Chinese government, via the Xinhua News Agency, dismissed Lee Tse-dhung, publisher of the Hong Kong based *Wen Wei Po* newspaper (in which Xinhua has a holding interest) and replaced him by the obedient Chen Bo-jian. In various articles, Lee had supported the pro-democratic movement in China, while Chen opposed it. According to Lee Yi, publisher of the journal *Nine-*

ties, "this shows that the one-land two-systems concept is actually a farce. We have the choice of giving no news or acting as the mouthpiece of Beijing. Those organs which report the news had better disappear."

In August 1994, the president of Giordano Holdings Ltd., Jimmi Lai, was pressured to give up his dominant role in the $120 million company he had founded. Being also a publisher, he had called Prime Minister Li Peng in his magazine *NEXT* a "nincompoop," "slave master," "monster," and "shame of the Communist Party."

In 1993, Martin Lee, the head of the pro-democratic party, was labeled by the pro-Chinese faction in the legislature as subversive and counter-revolutionary. He was informed that because of this he could not continue in the legislation after 1997. When Lee, a distinguished lawyer himself, looked for a law firm to take the matter to court, eighteen of the leading law firms of Hong Kong declined for fear of displeasing Beijing.

On 6 June 1991, the Red Chinese government rejected the Bill of Rights, which the Parliament of Hong Kong had passed a few days earlier. On taking over power in the colony in 1997, that law would be abolished, they said. In January 1994, Beijing announced that on 30 June 1997, the day Britain transfers power in the colony to China, it will dissolve the legislature and other elected bodies. All laws will be reviewed by the People's National Congress, and after the election victory of the pro-democracy Democratic party in September 1995, the Chinese government said that it will annul the election after taking over power in July 1997. On the other hand, the Beijing government will inherit rules from the British, which were not abolished before signing the Sino-British treaty: censorship of television, curtailing the right to demonstrate, collection of money for political purposes, and police control for political entities.

John Major and his government still can decide whether they will follow in Churchill's tradition and hand over millions of human beings against their will to a totalitarian state of violence. They can also denounce the imperialistic colonialism which disregards human beings and bring about a renaissance in the homeland of democracy so that all human beings of all races will be equal, not only in words but also in truth. In the case of Hong Kong, that means taking a new line. In any case, the treatment of the Hong Kong people is an issue for all Europeans and their political institutions in the European Community.

The Marxist-Leninist philosophy of Mao, Chu en-Lai, Deng, Zao Zi-yang, Li Peng, and their party cadres conflicts with the basic ethical principles out of which the thousand-year-old Chinese culture has grown. The materialistic Western concept of communism is a rape of the self-perception of the Chinese and of their view of their own country based on the teachings of Lao-tse and Kung-tse (Confucius). For the Chinese, the world forms part of the divine universe and man is a reflection of the perfect harmony of the universe—an image of God, as Christians would say. The purpose of human existence, and thus man's most important task in this world, is to find the divine world order and incorporate himself into it. Consequently, human beings who only think of themselves, follow their own particular interests, and have no regard to the common good are saboteurs of the implementation of divine realization on earth. Kung-tse categorically rejected violence as a tool of the state order. Like Lao-tse, he believed that the selfish motives within man can be influenced and overcome in order to arrive at a harmonious human society.

According to the Chinese view of culture, it follows that I, too, am Chinese because the definition of a Chinese is not someone who has particular racial and national characteristics, but somebody who attempts to find his place in the divine world order. The concept of the central kingdom (with an emperor as the son of heaven) has arisen out of that philosophy, as has the classification of all human beings into the categories of Chinese and barbarians. According to that view, Deng Li-Peng and his consorts are not Chinese but barbarians. Not only do they fail to represent the real Chinese people, but they are its worst enemies who are trying to eliminate tradition and human substance. Applying Chinese criteria, I would also number James Baker, the American secretary of state, among the barbarians. I listened to him when he spoke of the Chinese orientation toward Western values, which had, unfortunately, been interrupted (but not brought to an end) by events in Tiananmen Square, and I wondered what values he was referring to. Did he mean the concept of the unbridled Western devotion to personal pleasure, with its consequences including drug abuse, AIDS, millions of divorces and abortions, the dissolution of family lives, cupidity, and racism—to name only a few of the achievements of our social chaos—or was he referring to our democratic formalism, which grants each individual the right to vote, although in fact that right is used by a diminishing number of people? If Chinese society grew out of the basic cell of the family/tribe, is our society (with its sexual lust and destroyed families) an example for China to follow?

If Chinese youth elevate the Statue of Liberty into a symbol, they are ultimately not seeking Western materialism, since they have had quite enough of the Eastern version. No, China is searching for its own identity and wishes to find itself based on its own tradition and culture, but under modern conditions. The Asian people, such as in India and Japan, who are culturally close to China, and all of the Western governments, must now help that country and its citizens and not abet its enemies in the government.

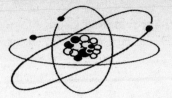

Communists Take Over
South Africa

The Country

From reading and listening to reports in recent years about the Republic of South Africa, Westerners must have gotten the impression that there is a black majority represented by the African National Congress; and that its leader, Nelson Mandela, had confronted the apartheid white minority government in the quest for justice and democracy. Western policy towards South Africa was based on this black/white confrontation concept, and used economic muscle and devastating sanctions to force the Boer government to yield power to the black majority. On the surface, this policy seems to have been successful. Mandela is president of the South African Republic, the apartheid laws have been abolished, and the whites have lost their hold on power. After the first free election in the history of the country (or so goes the success story), a multiracial democracy has been established. There is a new South Africa. Hallelujah!

This view of the situation, however, is misleading to say the least. The new South Africa is no newer than Germany was after Hitler took over. The issue in either case was never majority rule and democracy, but power. Racial injustice only served as a cover for the bid for power. Power manipulators never work for the common good, but only look after themselves. The Boers at least produced and made South Africa the most prosperous nation on the continent. Millions of black people entered (illegally) from the surrounding countries to find work. South Africa produced 77 percent of the Gross Domestic Product, 77 percent of the electricity, 87 percent of the grain, 70 percent of the corn, and 67 percent of the sugar cane in the whole African continent. It has the largest known reserves of gold (with 35 percent of the world's output), chromium, platinum, vanadium, manganese and andalusite, and substantial deposits of coal, uranium, diamonds, iron ore, zirconium, titanium, feldspar, nickel, and phosphates. Western industry depends on South African strategic minerals. Together, Russia and South Africa could strangle Western economies.

In the whole of Africa, internal politics are based on tribal structures. There are ten major black tribes in South Africa with at least fifty-seven languages and dialects. Many of these tribal peoples are fiercely independent, and it would be a big mistake not to take this into account.

Of the nearly 39 million people of the Republic, 74.2 percent are black; 14.1 percent are white; the Colored population, which arose from contact between the original Khoikhoi (Hottentot) tribes of the Cape, the early European settlers, slaves imported from the East, and later Black peoples, make up 8.2 percent; and the rest, 2.5 percent, are Asians. There is, interestingly, an important Israeli community. Sources of population figures per ethnic groups differ, and it is not easy to reconcile the different statistics published by various institutions. The following, though, should give a fair picture of the variety of black South Africans. The Zulu tribe, with 8 million people, is the largest ethnic group, comprising 27.6 percent of the black or 20.5 percent of the total population. The Xhosa, with 16.5 percent of the population, is the second biggest black ethnic group; then there are the North Sotho, the South Sotho, the Tswana, the Shangaan/Tsonga, the Swazi, the South Ndebele, the North Ndebele, and the Venda. The 3.2 million Colored make up the fourth largest ethnic group, the majority of them living in the Western Cape Province. Of the about 1 million Asians, 98 percent are Indians, and the rest are Chinese. Most live in Natal.

Each ethnic group has its own cultural identity, language, and social system. (According to the first census of the country in 1904, the population of the country consisted of 3,491,056 blacks, 1,116,806 whites, and 567,962 Colored for a total of 5,175,824.) The whites are divided into two groups: The African-speaking Boers (58 percent) and the English-speaking British descendents. Considerable numbers of immigrants from Portugal, Italy, Greece, Germany, France, and Scandinavia have integrated into both groups but primarily into the English speaking community. As long as apartheid has existed, there has been outspoken white opposition to it. In 1995 the Boers are divided in various political camps and without effective all-embracing leadership. Their unrelenting hatred of the British for destroying their independence in the nineteenth century and their fear of losing their identity have been at the heart of all of South Africa's problems.

According to a survey by the Institute of Race Relations published in May 1995, 66.5 percent of the population is Christian. According to Professor Dons Kritzinger, director of the Institute of Missiological Research at the University of Pretoria, the percentage is 77 percent. Like the Christians in Germany before and during Hitler's reign and the Christians of today in Western countries, their concepts are irrelevant to the power struggle and no match for the godless.

The African National Congress (ANC) is Xhosa dominated. Mandela is a Xhosa and so are most blacks in key positions. Twenty-nine of the fifty-six members of the National Executive of the ANC who were elected in July 1991 are card-carrying Communist party members. Most of the rest hide their party affiliation or call themselves Marxists-Leninists or Socialists. The ANC was founded in 1912 and was originally a democratic institution dedicated to the rights of black people. It was hijacked in the seventies by Communists who continued with the same language but introduced violence into the program. They have used the organization and the black people for their own power aspirations ever since. Many rights movements around the world have been taken over this way by the radical Left including in the United States.

Mandela does not speak for black South Africa. No Xhosa speaks for the Zulus and vice versa, no Sotho for the Tswana, no Zulu for the Venda, and so on. The idea of one black majority is a projection of Western concepts, unrelated to the reality of Africa.

The leader of the Zulus is Mangosuthu Buthelezi. Western politicians have mostly treated him as a nonperson. Our media has either ignored him or portrayed him as an ambitious rival to Mandela, an obstacle to progress. He is neither. I know him quite well. We are friends, and whenever I go to South Africa, I meet with him. He is a statesman, a Christian, and a democrat guided by principle. He refused to negotiate with the white government as long as Mandela was in prison and he worked tirelessly for Mandela's release. Mandela "thanks" him by trying to get him out of his and the Communist party's way—dead or alive.

While in the traditional tribal areas there is no doubt about who exercises authority, this is different in the black townships. There are millions of uprooted, most of them young, people who have been severely hit by the recession caused by economic sanctions. They have thus been pushed into the radical camp of Mandela and the ANC. The sanctions did the same to them as the Versailles treaty did to the German unemployed in the twenties. Those people in their desperation thought that Hitler would save them. In the townships, the battle for control was (and is!) raging, not between blacks and whites, but among blacks. It is there that the African National Congress has its strongholds, maintained to a large extent through intimidation by brute force: necklacing, assassinations, and similar actions. About sixteen hundred black opponents were killed by necklacing (putting a burning tire around the neck) by the African National Congress in the years preceding the elections: thirty-three alone in May, June, and the first days of July 1992 according to figures released by the police.

Half of the weapons used in violent attacks were firearms and explosives. The Soviet AK-47 was the most-used firearm, followed by shotguns. This points in the direction of the ANC, since only they were supplied by the Soviet Union with Soviet weapons. The Zulus have no such weapons. The Zulu police guarding the entry to Buthelezi's headquarters in Ulundi were unarmed (as I observed) when I was there. Ten percent of all deaths in the six years since violence began were attributed by the South African Institute of Race Relations to necklacing and burning. Only 18 percent of weapons used were pangas, knives, or axes. Of 176 people killed during February 1991, the cause of death was reported by the authorities in 87 cases: 64 people were shot (74 percent), 16 were hacked (18 percent), and 7 were stabbed (8 percent). Dr. Gavin Woods from the Inkatha Institute pointed out that traditional weapons have no part in shooting or hacking, and spears are only one of many weapons which can be used for stabbing. He was trying to establish the fact that the violence is not, as normally reported by the media, traditional tribal warfare. It is an attack by well-armed revolutionaries on their opponents.

These attacks and assassinations have continued unabated after the elections in KwaZulu-Natal. Between 1984 and 1995 "over 400 of our leaders and office bearers have (since) been murdered in a systematic plan of targeted assassination, and over 11,000 members and supporters of the IFP have lost their lives in this low intensity civil war,"[1] stated Buthelezi on 22 July 1995 at the twentieth anniversary conference of the IFP, which was attended by sixteen ambassadors from Europe, America, Asia, and Africa. Only two weeks earlier, two Zulu leaders, Rev. David Zondi and the uncle of a tribal chief, were murdered. Shortly before the election in March 1994, fifty-seven Zulus who demonstrated peacefully in front of the Shell House in Pretoria were killed by ANC security guards. Mandela admitted that he personally gave the order to shoot. To this day there has been no legal repercussion, and there was of course no coverage by the media.

The Election

The stage for the elections was set in March 1995 when the ANC/NP alliance overthrew the governments of Bophuthatswana and Ciskei, in violation of international law. Bophuthatswana was economically the fastest growing country in Africa. The democratically elected president, Lucas Mangope, and his equally freely elected Parliament were deposed of, and the population was distributed in crassest imperialist style to different South African provinces—without being asked of course. The army then received orders from Democrat de Klerk to bring down Buthelezi and KwaZulu—but the army leaders refused. The Associated Press described the process of liquidating the opposition by force as a victory for democracy-loving forces.

There were no free and honest elections on 27 April 1995, as were heralded by Western governments and media. There is no democratic election by counting votes. Massive fraud led to a situation in which the main parties agreed to accept a negotiated result which averted bloodshed. I asked Buthelezi why he had accepted this procedure. "The alternative would have been civil war," he answered. That civil war, however, could still break out.

The election boycott of about 1 million white conservatives can only be described as an incredibly idiotic suicide measure.

The "independent" Election Commission consisted (with the exception of one person) of people affiliated with the ANC. The ANC therefore knew that they would win in any case, which explains the absence of violence during the days of voting. There were 40 million voting permits for 21.7 million voters. One South African intelligence report even speaks of 97 million. Nevertheless, quite a number of polling stations (especially in Natal and Transvaal) remained without ballots. In Natal, twice as many votes were cast as there were voters. The ANC admitted to having brought people from Transkei to vote in Natal. On the other hand, 1.1 million ballots got "lost" on the way to Pretoria. The Freedom Front stated that 147,000 votes for them are missing. Hundreds of thousands of ballots printed in England were found in unopened boxes, premarked for ANC candidates. There were no voting lists and there was therefore no control. It is estimated that 2 million of the approximately 4 million illegal immigrants (mainly from Mozambique) voted for the ANC—which generously distributed Temporary Voter Identity Cards to them—an idea of Communist leader Joe Slovo.

Contrary to the stipulations of the South African Constitution (Section 101), the Communists registered not for their own party but for the ANC. The de Klerk government allowed this fraud to happen, which alone and by itself makes the whole election illegal. It is estimated that the Communist party counts on the backing of 1 percent of the population. When the new government was formed after the elections, sixteen of the twenty-eight ANC members in it were Communists. There are fifty of them in the National Assembly and quite a number in each regional Parliament.

The British "Intelligence Digest" estimated in 1992 that in the last ten years the ANC had received about 500 million pounds ($750 million) from foreign sources. Of this, $80 million came from the U.S. government alone that same year. Other financial sponsors include the Swedish government, American foundations, German churches, and the Libyan head of state, Momar Ghadafi. "The London Financial Times, The Economist and the Wall Street Journal, all have estimated that over the past 12 years the ANC must have banked some 5.5 to 6 billion Rands" (about $2 billion),[2] writes the South African journalist Aida Parker. I asked Buthelezi what international support he had received over the years. "None," he answered. The only organization which backs him is the German Konrad Adenauer Foundation.

U.S. Ambassador William Lacy Swing, who was later transferred to Haiti to supervise the ouster of Cedras and the installation of Aristide, installed offices in his embassy for the ANC/SACP leadership: Nelson Mandela, Walter Sisulu, Cyril Ramaphosa, Jacob Zuma, Joe Slovo, Thabo Mbeki, Chris Hani, Siphiwe Nyanda, "Red Ronnie" Kasrils, Gillian Marcus, and Raymond Mhlaba. They were given access to CIA communications, as well as computer and intelligence facilities.

Outside intervention into the internal affairs of South Africa, under the pretext of helping the democratic process, determined the outcome of the elections long before they took place. No Western country would have accepted anything of this sort within their own borders. Nevertheless, they applauded what was presented to them as progress to freedom, democracy, and justice. They were hopelessly deluded.

What does it mean to be brainwashed? It means, first of all, that you are not aware of it. You believe a lie to be truth because it is presented to you as such. The consequence is that you live in an unreal dream world. Most Western people are painting their cabins while the ship goes down. Many Germans, but not all, accepted the destroyer Hitler as a saviour. Many Americans and Western people, but not all, accept the destroyers—Mandela, Gorbachev, Allende, Aristide, and some of their own leaders of the same ilk—as honest democrats.

The Takeover

The main architect of the Communist march to power was Joe Slovo, a Lithuanian Jew and KGB colonel. He was for many years the secretary general of the South African Communist party and Housing minister in the first Mandela cabinet before he died of cancer. This brilliant but ruthless strategist, part of a global network, had no match in the narrow-minded and divided white establishment of opportunists. De Klerk surrendered to him. I suspect that de Klerk has been bought, like many others. With an estate in Spain, a pension as a former president and a salary as a vice-president (in total 884,343 Rand per year which is nearly $242,000), he has it made whatever happens. If he really were interested in justice, he could have worked with the moderate black leaders a long time ago. Slovo's concept, and that of his comrades, is to make South Africa the springboard to the restoration of Soviet global power. De Klerk and his fellow opportunists provided them with the means to do so.

The shaping of the Interim Constitution at the end of 1993, which led to elections and to the Mandela government, was the result of an agreement between the ANC and the governing National party. The Inkatha Freedom Party (IFP) headed by Buthelezi, which had always more than double the membership of the ANC, did not participate because its concepts of a federal structure for South Africa were disregarded.

There is a fundamental difference in the philosophies of free market-oriented Buthelezi and his allies (who want a federal state with limited central power, much like the Republicans in the United States) and the Socialist-Communist Mandela grouping (who want all the power and control in their hands at the center as established by the Apartheid government, much like the Democrats). The ANC has always justified violence and never renounced the use of force. As we have seen, the violence was mostly directed at other blacks. Mandela has always called for sanctions against his own people as a means to destroy the white government, thus making the country ripe for revolution. It is well to remember that, according to Alexander Solzhenitsyn, anyone who once proclaimed violence as his method must inexorably choose the lie as his principle. The Douglas Commission, entrusted by the International Freedom Foundation to investigate the ANC detention centers, compared them to Nazi concentration camps and to the Soviet Gulag. (Of course the ANC had its own camps outside of South Africa during its outlaw years.) According to the head of the commission, R.S Douglas, "the saga of the ANC/SACP in exile is one of tyranny, terror, brutality, forced labor in concentration camps and mass murder . . . a systematic policy of depraved brutality and persecution against their own members in exile."[3] Communist Joe Modise, a transport worker by profession principally responsible for those camps, was minister of defense in the first Mandela cabinet. His deputy, "Red Ronny" Kasrils, also a Communist, was second in command in the supervision of the camps. Both these men resemble strongly the Nazi concentration camp commander of Buchenwald, Karl Otto Koch. Buthelezi on the contrary, always against the sanctions, practiced nonviolent resistance to the apartheid regime in the tradition of Mahatma Ghandi.

After the Interim Constitution agreement was signed, Slovo reported to the Central Committee of the South African Communist party on 20 November 1993. Published in *The African Communist*, no. 136, Fourth Quarter, 1993 he proclaimed "a famous victory." "We engaged in negotiations with a revolutionary purpose," he wrote. "Negotiations are a terrain of struggle. . . . The negotiated package . . . is a famous victory. It represents . . . the culmination of decades of struggle."

UCANEWS, the newsletter of the United Christian Action, summarized Slovo's report:

Under the title: "The Negotiated victory" Slovo declared "I can say without hesitation that we got pretty much what we wanted." He then listed some of the Communist party victories as:

1. The acceptance of a two stage process where the final constitution will be drawn up only after the election.

2. A strong central government with overriding financial and military powers over the regions.

3. "We have won the battle against federalisation."

4. "We have also won the case for the re-incorporation of the TVBC states . . ."

5. The rejection of special majorities for decision making in a future government.

6. Obtaining substantial influence in the Independent Electoral Commission and the Independent Media Commission.

7. "Breaking the regime's monopoly over public media."

8. A land Restitution (confiscation) mechanism.

9. Deadlock breaking mechanisms to bypass the two-thirds majority requirement.

10. The removal of Afrikaan as one of the two official languages.

Slovo cautioned his fellow communists that "what has come out of Kempton Park (the site of the negotiations) is only a mountain of paper. The critical question now is implementation . . . we must provide the right with an option short of armed resistance. This involves dialogue and a strategy to divide them."[4]

When Slovo spoke of a "two-stage approach" he meant that the ANC makes a promise for the future without having the intention to keep it, in order to get an immediate advantage. So Mandela, de Klerk, and Buthelezi signed an agreement a few days before the elections on behalf of their respective parties, according to which international mediation would be sought for establishing a federal structure for South Africa in the final constitution. Because of the agreement, the Inkatha Freedom party took part in the election. Mandela, of course, does not keep his word. There will never be mediation if he gets his way; instead of it there is an all-out attack on Buthelezi and the independence of the Zulu nation. The figure head king was bought and now the attempt is underway to buy the tribal chiefs also, so as to separate them from Buthelezi. Divide and conquer.

Defamation and character assassination are part of this power strategy. An internal ANC Commission Report on Strategy and Tactics of June 1985 called Chief Buthelezi a counter-revolutionary who has to be exposed as such and be deprived of his social base. Another ANC document of the year 1992, "The Road to Victory, The Path to Power," states: "He (Buthelezi) remains properly the most dangerous enemy the movement has. (He) remains a festering sore which could develop into a dangerous growth if not destroyed immediately. Our strategy should be to place him under unbearable pressure and to continually seek ways and means of discrediting him locally and internationally . . . our media have played a useful role." The document also makes clear that the overriding aim of the SACP is "the ultimate transformation of South Africa into a true socialist state."[5]

The worldwide Buthelezi defamation campaign is carried forward by thousands of fellow travellers especially in religious organizations. In the IBM notice of the 1992 Annual Meeting and Proxy Statement one can find under point 4 "Stockholder Proposal on South Africa" the framework of an attempt by owners of 221,520 shares to force IBM to cut all business with South Africa:

> IBM employees and religious organizations are sponsoring this resolution. Five hundred sixty IBMers from Europe, Japan and the United States signed a similar resolution in 1991; 368 IBMers signed in 1990; 91 in 1989; and 6 in 1988. . . . The white minority maintains rule not by the free choice of South African citizens, but by massive violence—unrestrained killings by government police forces, death squads, and black vigilante followers of KwaZulu Bantustan Minister Gatsha Buthelezi, a key official in the apartheid government.

One can observe how the campaign gained ground over the years and I wonder how many annual meetings of other companies had similar proposals. I would be interested to know which religious organizations put forward such a blatant lie. If the promoters call themselves Christians, they are not. They are liars.

Buthelezi stated in a speech on 22 July 1995, "The IFP believes that South Africa shall be organized in a federation of Provinces. Provinces shall operate as the primary government of the people, and only those powers which cannot be adequately and properly exercised at a provincial level should be devolved upwards to the federal government, for federalism promotes political pluralism, allowing different parties to be in power at the same time in different regions and levels of government." This of course does not suit the all-power aspirations of Mandela and the ANC. "It can be fairly said," continues Buthelezi, "that the ANC's main goal is to establish a single monolithic center of political power, under its control to the exclusion of any other source of autonomous power. In fact, the ANC's hostility against autonomous power extends both to the power exercised by Provinces, as well as to the power exercised by institutions of civil society."[6] That shows Mandela's Nazi mentality because we have seen the same in Nazi and Soviet Germany.

The end of apartheid is not just the result of Western sanctions and ANC violence, but of the peaceful resistance of millions of moderate blacks who opposed a stupid and arrogant government. It is primarily the Western media which have distorted the picture, portraying Mandela and the ANC as the main protagonists. "Non-violence and negotiation is what the real black struggle for liberation is all about,"[7] Buthelezi had said in 1991. He, like the majority of the black people, have opposed sanctions and desperately tried to convince Western leaders that above all they are hurting the black majority, whom they pretend to help. "Sanctions are a recipe for violence and despair," he stressed, "and they are the enemy of all who want this country to emerge as a united, non-racial, multi-party, free-enterprise democracy."[8]

The East German Communists, who opposed Hitler and sat in his concentration camps, were not democrats simply because they were anti-Nazi. They wanted the power the Nazis had. Neither is Mandela a democrat because he is anti-apartheid. He and his comrades want the power. Honecker, the former East German party boss, and his colleagues established a totalitarian police state after the Nazis were defeated. Mandela is in the process of doing the same. His calls for sanctions against his own country was a typical Communist tactic to increase the suffering and unrest among the population, so that they are willing to accept any alternative to the status quo. Would it have been right for German resistance leaders during World War II to have called for the bombing of their own civilian populations in Germany while they were safe in Switzerland, in order to destroy the evil Nazi regime? No bomb would hit them in Switzerland. Neither does millionaire Mandela suffer from economic sanctions—but the poor do. He is a traitor.

Philosophically, Western democracies should be on the side of the Buthelezi forces. It is an astounding phenomenon that, contrary to our professed democratic and free-market creed and contrary to our interests, the anti-democratic ANC and Mandela have always received the limelight, as well as political and financial support from the West, while Buthelezi scarcely exists as far as the media are concerned. Contrary to the essence of democracy, Western leaders disregarded the wishes of the black majority, and contrary to Christian teachings (which they pretend to adhere to) they institute and support a policy based on hatred, ruining the existences of millions of black people and nearly destroying the only country which could make a difference to a dying continent.

That should make us think, but it doesn't. We are too absorbed with ourselves. The West has crippled the economy of a country which otherwise would have had the strength to save the population of Somalia from starvation, to mention only one consequence. As a result, hundreds of thousands, if not millions, of people die while we appease our conscience with inadequate humanitarian aid, still refusing to face the truth. What is staggering is the hypocrisy and ruthlessness of Western governments who have no solutions to the racial and ethnical divisions in their own countries, but force their poisonous medicine down the throat of another country, destroying it in the process. The parliaments and governments which have promoted this policy will have to face the evil they set in motion. The thousands and thousands of misguided Western anti-apartheid campaigners will have to respond to the consequences of their government's immoral and destructive actions, which they made possible, in the same way as I had to make myself responsible for the atrocities of the German Nazi government. Yes, I do indeed compare Western policy with Nazi policy. To make myself crystal clear, I am not saying that Western leaders are Nazis, but I do say that their policies are based on the same evil that was at the heart of nazism: hatred, the arrogant indifference of the strong towards helpless fellow human beings, and lust for power. It doesn't matter whether one is acting out of one's own hatred or the hatred of others, the result is the same. Love does not produce misery and destruction, as the sanctions did.

"We shall achieve victory through a combination of mass political action and organized revolutionary violence," Oliver Tambo, president of the ANC, had stated in 1985 in the Marxist magazine *New International*. The slogan "power to the people," Tambo explained, "means one thing and one thing only. It means we seek to destroy the power of apartheid tyranny and replace it with popular power. To march forward must mean that we advance against the regime's organs of power, creating conditions in which the country becomes increasingly ungovernable. As strategists we must select for attack those parts of the enemy administration system which we have the power to destroy."[9] Jack Barnes, president of the American Socialist party, elaborated in the same edition of the *New International*. "It will take a mighty battle to break the ties that bind the U.S. government to the South African regime. Breaking those ties is the task of the people of the United States," Barnes explains. "It is a task of the communist vanguard in this country."[10] Additionally, his plan foresaw an international campaign to free Mandela and get American investors to withdraw from South Africa. The success of this strategy is remarkable. It is worth mentioning that Barnes' concept, the program of a man who presides over a party of about one thousand members, prevailed over the wishes of Ronald Reagan, president of the United States of America with 240 million people. That again should make us think.

Buthelezi always reached out to the whites as fellow South Africans whose services to the country are indispensable. His moral stature was what impressed me most when I discussed the situation with him in Ulundi. There was no hint of hatred, revenge or desire to make the white man pay for the humiliation he and his people had suffered at their hands. He is a Christian such as I have rarely seen among political leaders.

"From my perspective of life," he explains, "I have to constantly cling to the conscious knowledge that it is Christ who directs the affairs of South Africa and that it is He who is leading this country to its divinely appointed ends. It is Christ's kingdom on earth that we should be striving for."[11] Referring to the West he says,

> There is a blindness to South African revolutionaries' real endeavors to bring about the ungovernability of South Africa by developing a people's war. There is a blindness to the real brutality of punitive economic sanctions against the South African government which could well be thrusting the poorest of the poor beyond the reach of life itself in the future. There is an austerity of love in the theologians..., who see God as involved in a vicious backlash of the oppressed and who is there with revolutionaries who are making ordinary men, women and more tragically children, the cannon fodder of their campaigns.[12]

Apartheid is finished. How the wounds which discrimination, brutality, and injustice of that system have created will be healed is up to the South Africans. But the focus has shifted from the black-white confrontation to the battle between the different black groups and their allies as to how the structures of the new country will be and what philosophy will prevail. To believe that a bunch of revengeful Communists, fellow travellers, and opportunists can unite the country and lift it upwards is absurd.

Chaos in Black Africa

The picture presented by southern Africa today is sad. There is internal warfare and natural disaster combined with incompetence and corruption of mostly Marxist government leaders like Kaunda, Nyere, Mugabe, Mobutu and others who have driven Angola, Zambia, Zimbabwe, Tanzania, Zaire and Mozambique to the brink of disaster. All of these countries have received massive injections (in the billions!) of Western aid only to find themselves in catastrophic conditions. Most of the rest of African countries fall into the same category. While Zimbabwe's economy grew by 52.3 percent between 1975 and 1980 under Ian Smith, the braggart Mugabe, who belongs to the tribe of the Shona, managed to achieve a negative growth of 9.5 percent in the first five years after he took power in 1980. His main effort was to consolidate his Marxist one-party system by eliminating any threat to his power by the minority Ndebele/Kalanga tribe. Right at the beginning of his regime, the Germans were falling all over themselves to provide him with economic aid, which enabled him to maintain his personal lifestyle. Kaunda in Zambia was even more successful than he. During the same five years Zambia's GNP fell by 40.7 percent. At least Nyere was courageous enough to admit at the end of his term that "Tanzania is poorer than twenty years ago." He did not go so far, however, as to draw a connection between this fact and his leadership. Neither has the Western taxpayer realized that his government has been taking money out of his pocket to pour out hundreds of billions of dollars to Marxist regimes around the world, reaping nothing but economic and ecological chaos. And they continue to do it.

South Africa heads in the same direction. The new South Africa is as new as was Germany after Hitler assumed power by democratic elections. The country is in the second phase in the transition to a Socialist totalitarian state. The Communist consolidation of power by the end of 1995 is well advanced. The armed forces, security services, and police are in their hands and are slowly being transformed into an instrument of oppression. The judicial system (under Communist Dullah Omar, the minister of justice) will administer the same kind of justice as we had in Nazi Germany and Soviet Russia: make opposition illegal. The Constitutional Court is packed with ANC/SACP affiliates, and as we have seen in the United States, it is not too difficult to transform a constitution to achieve the opposite of its original meaning if you know how to manipulate words.

ANC's Five Year Reconstruction & Development Plan promoted by Mandela during the election campaign has a price tag of $1.5 billion. Mandela promised for the five-year period 1.5 million new homes, electrification of 400,000 homes a year; clean water, sanitation, health care, ten years of universal free education and an affordable telephone for everyone. Pure demagoguery. The South African economy, with a work force which is considered to have one of the lowest productivity rates in the world, will be utterly unable to comply with that target. So one of Mandela's principal tasks will be to make Western governments pay the bill.

Before both Houses of Congress on 6 October 1994, Mandela, presenting himself as the liberator of the oppressed, articulated the Socialist-Communist concept for the New World Order. Most of those who listened and gave him standing ovations, I am afraid, mistook it for enlightened expressions for the progress of democracy. He expects the United States, all Western countries, and the international financial institutions to create "a world of democracy, peace and prosperity." Redistribution of wealth on a global scale (with the United Nations as a principal vehicle) is the substance of that concept. A man who, together with his comrades, has been busy destroying his country for the sake of his own power, wants others to foot the bill. He can only be matched by the ignorance of those who promoted his cause.

The question has been asked: who controls the South African Communists and therewith the strategic minerals? Are they on their own? Is it the KGB in Moscow? Or do Western financial centers and big business pull the strings? After all, it was Gavin Relly, then chairman of the Anglo-American Corporation, which owns about half of all companies registered at the Johannesburg stock exchange (on instruction of patriarch Harry Oppenheimer), who in 1985 brought a delegation of South African businessmen to Lusaka, the capital of Zambia, to meet with the ANC leadership. The London Rhodesian Corporation, Lonrho (under Tiny Rowland), the Rockefeller Foundation and countless Anglo-American companies, foundations, and banks contributed millions of dollars to the ANC cashbox. Tiny Rowland was quoted, saying, "As far as I am concerned, I don't mind if Africa becomes communist—all the better. Communists are able to manipulate people, but companies have to remain in capitalistic hands. Capitalist and Communist leadership works glove in hand."[13]

What is the future of South Africa? Mangosuthu Buthelezi says the following: "We in South Africa have a great opportunity to establish for the first time, a true modern and yet true African State which will harmonise Westernised first-world realities with African traditional realities in a common framework of social and economic development marked by freedom, tolerance, and mutual respect. This goal will either be achieved the next year (1996) or it will be forgone for many decades to come."[14]

By 1995, within one year after the ANC took over power, South Africa is sinking into chaos. Whites are leaving the country in droves. Affirmative action furthermore makes incompetence flourish and assures diminishing productivity and a reduced tax base. Criminality is pervading everything. A visitor of a friend of mine was shot dead in front of his house by the thieves who tried to steal his car. "The police is practically nonexistent," my friend told me. Dr. Lloyd Voglemen, head of the Center for the Study of Violence and Reconciliation stated: "In 1994 there were more than 800,000 violent crimes, including 18,000 murders, 67,000 armed robberies, 150,000 serious assaults, 31,000 rapes and 55,000 automobiles were stolen."[15] In Johannesburg alone there are 300 organized crime syndicates. The city is considered today to be the most dangerous place in the world. The country is reaping the consequences of the violence that the ANC (financed by western Christian churches and governments) has been sowing.

Two white homosexuals were the first ones to die of AIDS in 1982. The disease spread into the black townships only in 1987. According to an estimate by the Department of Health,

566,000 South Africans were HIV-positive at the end of 1993. In October 1993 Dr. Keith Heiman of the National Council for Child and Family Welfare warned, according to a report in the "Aida Parker" newsletter, that South Africa could expect up to 12 million people dead of the disease within ten years. Additionally, tuberculosis is spreading. There were 804,000 recorded cases in 1990. More than 12 million people have dormant TB infection, estimates the SA Tuberculosis Association. The combination of the two infections could produce an avalanche of cases at the beginning of the next century which the health system will be unable to handle. It is already disintegrating because of incompetent Socialist government intervention, which leads to a growing number of doctors leaving the country. There is only one retinal (eye) doctor left in South Africa.

At the same time, the Mandela government is establishing close links with Cuba and Iran. The State Department is protesting. They see the danger that nuclear secrets could be passed on from South Africa to hostile nations. They should protest themselves and the Congress should take a close look at what has been going on in South Africa.

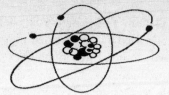

The New World Order Hoax

The New World Order is supposed to be the result of the cooperation of the two former superpowers, the United States of America and the Soviet Union, to ensure peace, stability, and order for the peoples of the world. The benefits promised to the individual by the promoters of this concept are precisely the same ones that the Marxists-Leninists have promised over the last few decades. The concept is based on the ignorance of the reality of human nature, as well as ignorance of the true nature of communism, seeing communism basically as a military threat to oneself and as an ineffective state-controlled economy, instead of understanding communism as a subversive, godless and destructive social force. Communism is threatening us from inside our own society and is already deeply embedded in the structures of Western societies.

The New World Order is a concept born out of Western materialism, promoted by Western governments to be imposed, very often, on other countries, irrespective of the desires of their people by economic muscle. It is the bourgeoise equivalent to the Marxist dream of a classless society, the advent of which is to signal the fulfillment of the historic evolution of mankind into a permanent state of happiness and prosperity, where none suffer exploitation by others and where the material needs of all are being met.

Both concepts, the Western and the Eastern, are anti-God, immoral if not amoral, contrary to human nature, and lead to the destruction of society. Blind mankind, preoccupied with itself, is moving closer to self-annihilation. The materialistic nature of the two concepts can be recognized by the fact that they are neutral to values of character and, contrary to common perception, the two concepts are not exclusionary. The West embraces amoral communism while declaring it dead. Whereas the Communist vision cites human dignity, equality, brotherhood, and social justice as the substance of its message of salvation. The New World Order, according to its promoters, is supposed to be based on freedom, democracy, and human rights. Both argumentations are false. In both cases, the facts are contrary to the pronouncements. Instead of brotherhood in the one side and liberty in the other there is brutal oppression and slavery. None grows out of the beliefs and convictions of the people concerned but is being forced upon them from above, from heartless bureaucrats who are interested primarily in their own status, and their vision is limited to the exterior concepts of power.

The Eastern concept is imposed by the force of arms, and because of it there are 1.25 billion human beings still living in subhuman conditions in totalitarian states. The Western version is imposed by the force of economic power, but arms are not excluded either. The United Nations, an international institution co-founded by Stalin and neutral to values of character, consisting of a majority of non-democratic members, is about to become an instrument of the promoters of the New World Order. After all, the promoters control the cash that everyone is so interested in obtaining.

In the Communist states people work principally to maintain the luxurious lifestyle of a few million rulers, the nomenclature. That has not changed very much over time. The New World Order is headed in the same direction. Since the elected representatives of the people in most democracies have engulfed their countries and future generations through their incompetence, greed and self-seeking in strangling debt-situations, taxes are likely to rise everywhere. They will rise not just to pay for the debt-service but also to pay elevated salaries to an international establishment, which to a great extent has no popular mandate but claims to guarantee stability and order. This development will also lead to slave states, in which people will have to maintain the ruling elite and adopt themselves in their thinking and acting to the line laid down from above and conveyed to them as "politically and morally correct" by the media, which are already busy confusing people and destroying fundamental moral values. In other words, a relative morality—Nazi morality—to serve the purposes of the state is already in the process of being established. The craving of people to be in line with the others and accommodate themselves with whatever is generally accepted is a stronger force than the orders of a dictator. Much of the perversion of today's society can be traced to this phenomenon. Life will be like it was in old Rome: "bread and games," which means pleasure and immorality, disguised as emancipation, for the ruled, who in turn will leave their rulers to their devices. Brainwashed with lies, people might even vote them into power.

The following are examples of the congruence of the two materialistic concepts:

• Alliance of Western democracies with Soviet leader Michael Gorbachev, an atheistic Marxist-Leninist.

• The West German government was still collaborating with the East German Communist leadership when the East German people were already on the streets protesting the same rulers.

• It is business as usual with the Communist leaders in China after the non-Communist Republic of China was expelled from the United Nations. The elimination of liberty in Tibet and the assassination of 1.2 million Tibetans matters as little as the expressed desire of vast numbers of the Chinese population congregating in Tianaman Square in 1989. As a permanent member of the Security Council, China participates in sanctioning other, smaller countries which are far less oppressive than itself.

• The British and Portuguese governments contract to deliver the people of Hong Kong and Macao to totalitarian China without consulting their subjects or letting the subjects participate in negotiations.

• Western governments allied themselves with Nelson Mandela and his Communist front organization, the African National Congress, and ruined the Republic of South Africa with economic sanctions under the pretext of helping the black population to gain their rights, ignoring the expressed protests of the vast majority of the same blacks, who wanted work and no sanctions. Their leaders were shunned and a Communist-dominated government installed.

• Western governments first allied themselves with Saddam Hussein and then with Hafez Assad, both leaders of ruthless and immoral totalitarian-type states in Iraq and Syria and then the U.S. government tries to force Israel to make peace with Assad, who is as reliable a partner as was Adolf Hitler.

There is a difference in the professed creed of the promoters of the two concepts: the Communists beginning with Gorbachev are atheists for whom no absolute morality exists. In their amorality they are true to themselves. Western democrats, to a large degree, are churchgoing Christians—at least they consider themselves as such. In fact, promoters of both concepts share the same disregard for the human dignity of other people, which they proclaim to defend. They subjugate others to an inhuman intellectual fantasia, which in the final analysis only serves the promoters. Their actions are diametrically opposed to the command of our Lord to love our neighbors as we love ourselves, which in turn is the consequence of the commandment to love God, our Father, above anything else. What I just said is not an expression of a disputable personal religious point of view, but rather the existential reality of this world. This truth can be denied, but it cannot be altered.

There is a fundamental irresponsibility, hypocrisy, and lawlessness in the approach of Western governments towards international affairs. Establishing arbitrary measures at great expenses around the world in the name of human rights through a lawless body like the United Nations is only one expression of this. What is being established is not universal law but relative morality being administered by a group of hypocrites and hypocritical nations. Western legality—and that means Western society—is based on the concept that everybody is the same before the law. Totalitarian states destroyed that concept. In totalitarian realm of power, they established a "legality" to serve the interest of the government where people were treated according to their usefulness to the state. Immoral Western governments are now destroying in international affairs the principle on which their societies are founded and which theoretically are still the rule of their own lands. If this trend is not reversed and if international relations are not being based on universal law— meaning that moral absolutes are followed and binding for all nations—then there is only one likely outcome from the policy of Western governments: global totalitarian rule. In the same way as embittered, sleeping, or indifferent Germans installed Adolf Hitler in 1933 and then could not get rid of him, so are embittered, sleeping or indifferent Americans and Europeans in the process of installing their own slavemasters. Some of the Nazi features are already in place in America and are being pushed by people, organizations, and lawmakers. And who do you think those totalitarian rulers who will emerge are going to be? Naturally this is hard to predict, but considering the speed of developments, my guess for the international scene is that able-bodied Mikel Gorbachev will reappear, maybe as the next secretary general of the United Nations. In America, the Clinton administration is preparing the way for totalitarian rule by establishing policies and putting thousands of embittered people, whose basic philosophy is class war, into key positions.

Bitterness, envy, hatred, power and greed are nothing but an expression of man's self-centeredness, his egotism. The German professor for constitutional law, Ernst von Hippel, wrote years ago:

> Egotism as a modern sickness of the soul has led in great parts of the Western world to a political situation which can be described as alienation by men from men. This resulted not only in the disintegration of old forms of community but in the abolition of community as such. Because selfishness as a normal attitude does not just destroy existing forms of community but prevents the formation of any community.

> The temporary task of Western society must be the overcoming of egoism by raising man above himself. When man recognizes his true nature as part of a higher order, he will realize that his true self is based on selflessness.

The Democratic-Bureaucratic Establishment

The Undefined Concept of Democracy

On 26 December 1991 the Islamic Salvation Front won an overwhelming victory in the first election round for the Algerian Parliament. It won 180 of the 231 contested seats. The second round for the same number of seats was scheduled to take place in January 1992. On 11 January Pres. Chadli Beadjedid resigned, the military formed a council of state, declared the election invalid, and cancelled the second round.

The Islamic Fundamentalists had made it clear before the elections that they were against democracy and did not have any intention of governing Algeria democratically if elected. The Marxist government of this one-party state had led the country towards bankruptcy in the thirty years of uninterrupted power. The military and their allies cited the need to save democracy as motivation for their action.

That raises two questions: first, whether there was a democracy to be saved; and second, whether the claim to save democracy justifies a military coup. Getting at it from a different angle, is it legitimate according to our understanding of democracy that an anti-democratic political force use the democratic process to destroy democracy? Is it democratic to observe the formal rules of democracy, which give the same rights to everybody, in order to deprive those who think differently of their rights once power has been achieved?

Gen. Augusto Pinochet and the military took up arms against Salvador Allende, the elected president of Chile, who had violated the constitution forty-six times and whose government was declared illegal by Congress, as well as by the Supreme Court. Who is the democrat, the president who got to his place because of votes or the general who ousted him to protect the rights of the people? What is the definition of a democrat? And is democracy exclusively a matter of procedures or do the characters and goals of those involved in the process play a role? Would it have been democratic or undemocratic if the German military leaders in 1933 had ousted the elected chancellor of the Reich, Adolf Hitler, and his Nazi cronies, who had been elected to the Reichstag even though the evil they perpetrated was still hidden and not yet proven in its magnitude? Or would it be more democratic to wait until a destroyed country and millions of people murdered make the point clear for everybody?

On 5 April 1992 the elected president of Peru, Alberto Fujimori, sent his troops into the streets, closed Parliament, dismissed a dozen judges of the Supreme Court, and declared a state of emergency with dictatorial powers for himself. This, he reasoned, was necessary to prevent the country from sinking into chaos. He was attempting to deal with the armed insurrection of the terrorist Shining Path, which had caused already twenty-five thousand dead and $22 billion in material damage, to save democracy. Peru did not have democracy, he argued, but "coimacracy" (*coima* is the spanish word for *bribe*). He explained that the corruption of a major part of the democratic establishment made solving the country's problems through the established channels of government impossible.

The Gross National Product per capita in Peru in 1975 was the same as that of Chile, one-third higher than Ecuador and double that of Paraguay, which at that time was the lowest in Latin America, according to Harvard professor Robert J. Barro. By 1990 the Peruvian Gross National Product per capita was less than half that of Chile, 20 percent less than that of Ecuador, and 10 percent below that of Paraguay. Violence and misery continued in Peru at the time of the coup. One of my sisters-in-law was held up at gunpoint three times, another one only two times, and when the terrorists blew up the power lines, as they routinely did, my mother-in-law had difficulty replacing what spoiled in the ice box. My brother-in-law took different routes to his factory each day because he was being threatened by the Shining Path. Nearly all of government certain tax income went to paying the salaries of the bloated bureaucracy, but if you need anything to be done, public servants generally don't move until they see extra cash.

More than 85 percent of the nearly seven thousand terrorists captured by the police in eleven years were set free for "lack of evidence" by the judges, thrown out by Fujimori. Every Peruvian knows what is involved. The preceding APRA government under Alan Garcia had accelerated the downslide of the country, being the first Peruvian government ever to touch the gold reserves in the Central Bank, but strangely enough, most of them—especially Garcia himself—had left government service in a solid personal financial position.

Eight-five percent of the population backed the action of their president who, when elected, was not a member of the political establishment but was president of the agricultural university. Part of the ousted members of Congress elected one of their group to be president and declared Fujimori to be "unconstitutional." Western democratic governments deplored the "destruction of democratic legitimacy," froze all financial assistance, and reduced contacts to the Peruvian government to the minimum working level, as I was told by the German Embassy.

The question here is, who is the democrat? Fujimori, because he has the backing of the majority of the people, or his counterpart Ramirez, because he was elected by the majority of the members of Congress; or as spokesman for Western democratic leaders who sanction the country, George Bush, because he knows so much about democracy, other people, and what they should do? The Peruvian people watched neighboring Chile under Pinochet take off economically, leaving them far behind. If what they know of democracy is only their experience of corruption in the establishment and misery for the ordinary people, how do we expect them to react? Do Western democrats have the answer to corruption? Fujimori certainly has changed

Peru for the better (in spite of Western democracies), established constitutional legitimacy, crushed the Shining Path, and started economic growth after years of decline.

Zviad Gamsakhurdia received an overwhelming majority when elected president of Georgia in the former Soviet Union. In January 1992, a military council ousted him after weeks of bloody fighting, the details of which are described in another chapter. He was accused of trying to establish a dictatorship. This action was a coup, but I know of no protests in the rest of the world. On the contrary, Secretary of State James Baker went to visit his friend, the new head of the government, Eduardo Schevardnaze, after the coup.

Contrast the Georgian coup to what happened in Haiti. When the elected president, Jean Claude Aristide, was accused of abuse of power and forced by the military in 1991 to leave his country, worldwide protests were the consequence. Sanctions were imposed to "restore democracy." Two years later the only result of this ultimate weapon of Western democracies is the deepening misery of the masses in this poorest country in the Western Hemisphere. The desperation and hopelessness of the people of Haiti is beyond description. We know of the thousands who tried to get into the United States only to be returned, but there are at least three hundred thousand refugees in the neighboring Dominican Republic causing hardship for that country also. We seem to be incapable of bringing solutions to any situation, and only make matters worse by our interventions. The re-installation of Aristide by military force is not going to solve any problem in that country. The corruption of the Right has been changed to the corruption of the Left.

On the other hand, nobody boycotts China anymore, although the leadership there liquidated its democratic movement in a bloody crackdown and keeps the population under its thumb. Nobody can have any doubt about the totalitarian nature of that regime. But business comes first, and according to the way the game is played in Washington and the other Western capitals, it "must be kept separately from politics," as the German foreign office explains. Instead of sanctions, China gets most-favored-nation status. The German government grants a low interest credit of $400 million to the Chinese to be used to build four container-ships in German shipyards. Haiti has nothing of this kind to offer. It seems that our passion for democracy depends on the trade volume or oil. This brings us to the next question: is the principle of democracy still a principle if their leading representatives apply it selectively according to their own interest, instead of applying the same moral criteria to every situation?

The majority leader of the House of Representatives, Richard Gephart, explained in April 1992 an initiative of his party to raise taxes: "This tax will take money from the rich which we will then pass on to the neglected middle class." He called this a measure to "stimulate" the economy. He, like the majority of his colleagues who sponsor this initiative, belong to the middle class. Bill Clinton is totally identified with this principle. Question: is it democratic when a majority takes advantage of a minority, or is it just pure theft? Is there a difference in achieving this result, taking the money from the rich and putting it into the pockets of the less rich, if it is done by vote instead of at gunpoint? And if a reader came to the conclusion that it is theft, what does that then say about our democracy?

In May 1992, 2.3 million German public servants went on strike. The difference between what was offered by the government as a salary raise and what the union demanded was 0.6 percent. In constantly changing locations, hospitals were reduced to emergency service, trains did not roll, airports were closed, garbage was not collected, schools did not function, mail was not delivered, and so forth. The union leaders issued communiques, which reminded me of World War II. The only difference was that at that time it said, "enemy ship sunk," now it was saying triumphantly, "three and a half million letters not delivered." Every citizen had to suffer because of the disconnected services and when the strike was over after nearly two weeks, the cost for the economy was several hundred millions of dollars, to be picked up by the same citizens, who had nothing to do with the dispute but had to pay taxes. The strikers gained the 0.6 percent difference. When in the United States, in June of the same year, the machinists of the railway system went on strike for higher wages and were sent back to work by Congress, I heard one worker complain about the violation of his constitutional right to strike. It had been estimated that a strike would have cost the U.S. economy, just pulling out of a recession, $1 billion a day.

Is a strike of this nature a democratic right, a legitimate procedure in our democracies? In this case I want to make my position clear: I do not think so. No constitution in the world can give a minority the right to harm the majority of their fellow citizen for their own financial benefit. The right to strike must have a limit and has to be defined anew. People who say they are democrats have to learn how to resolve their differences without harming others. I wonder what kind of personal relationships exist between the representatives of the public employers in Germany and the union leaders. Do they socialize, meet with their families, go out for dinner, etc., so that they are familiar with each other, respect the other and can iron out differences when they arise? Or, is the other side just the enemy in a class war situation? Strikes are a symptom of the self-seeking and the inward looking of social forces within our society. United efforts should be directed towards lifting the millions who are living in misery in the Third World. The indebtedness of the United States government reached $5 trillion at the beginning of 1996, thirteen times as high as it was in 1980. That is $20,000 per American citizen. The government's propositions to reduce the deficit cannot be taken seriously. We are heading for disaster. The debt service will soon be the biggest single item after the entitlement expenses in the federal budget. In addition, most states are struggling with immense problems because of their own budget deficits. California has been for years close to bankruptcy. The debt burden for each American, therefore, is considerably higher. The situation is much the same in all of Western democracies with the possible exception of Switzerland. The level of indebtedness may differ but the principle is the same. German federal government debt was one trillion marks in 1992, which means sixty-five hundred dollars per German citizen, and the states are in the same position as their American counterparts. Furthermore, the debts of the developing countries, including the Latin American democracies, were caused by the same Western democracies. It is they who provided the money, practically throwing it at them. Governments and international institutions dominated by the West were helped in their give-aways by equally insane banks.

After pumping hundreds of billions of dollars into the Eastern European Communist states, it became evident after the breakdown of the Socialist systems that all this money had no effect whatsoever in long-term economic benefits for the people. It only financed and prolonged the privileged lifestyle and rule of the immoral leadership (the nomenclature) and assisted them in their expensive global efforts to subvert our societies. At that time, the reason for the financing was the intent to lead those countries to a less aggressive and dangerous form of society and government. Now, the reasons are that we must not help them to fall back into their old aggressiveness. I am not saying that we are not called to help, but I am saying that we are going about it in the wrong and self-destructive way, as we have in the past, because the recipients of our money are the same crooked bureaucrats.

One must therefore ask whether democracy and financial mismanagement go hand in hand. Is it democratic when the elected representatives of the people as a rule spend huge amounts of money they do not have, burdening their own voters and putting future generations into financial chains? Is it democratic when Western countries actively contribute to the bankruptcy of other countries by applying the wrong medicine and lavishing money on self-seeking despots, who in turn use it to perpetuate the misery of ordinary people?

England is considered to be the first Western democracy, the country that developed the concept and practice of democracy, which later on was adopted by others, including Germany. What other name than schizophrenic, should I call an attitude that practices democracy at home but not with regard to colonies? For example, the people of Hong Kong were not given the right to decide their own fate but were being turned over to the rule of Communist China. Is the prime minister, who submits to democratic procedures at home yet applies dictatorial procedures in the colonies, a democrat or a dictator? This leads to the question of whether the concept of democracy applies only to the proceedings within a given country or also to the external relationship to the people of other countries? Do their expressed desires bear any relation to the actions of Western democrats?

We think of Augusto Pinochet of Chile as a dictator and Carlos Salinas de Gotari of Mexico as a democrat. Pinochet let himself be voted out of power, receiving still 45 percent of the vote, while Salinas de Gotari continued the tradition of his party, the Institutional Revolutionary party, and reached the presidential chair only through massive election fraud. When he left office, he was a rich man, but Mexico was in shambles. Pinochet inherited an economic mess but started Chile on the road to economic growth and made his country the envy of all Latin America. With our same twisted logic, we institute sanctions against Fujimori of Peru and install the non-democratic Emir of Kuwait (a real dictator in royal oil purple) in his office and declare triumphantly that the authorized war-aim of the United Nations has been achieved.

That brings us to the United Nations. The majority of the member nations, as well as those in the Security Council, are non-democratic. Murderous totalitarian states like Iraq, Libya, Syria, Cuba, Iran, or Zaire have the same privileges as Australia or Holland who apply democratic principles and respect, and protect the rights of others through their institutions and their law. Totalitarian Communist China is a permanent member of the Security Council with the right to veto, as was the totalitarian Soviet Union. An East German Communist even made it to the presidency of the Assembly. At that time his Wall-erecting crowd was not yet accused of criminal acts. Although those acts were committed in broad daylight, they resulted in nothing but pious declarations on our side. They were only declared criminals by the principled democracies after they were out of power and therefore unable to retaliate. The governments of the majority of the United Nations' members are in structural and flagrant violation of the Declaration of Human Rights, the "constitution" of the United Nations. However, they do not hesitate to denounce others and to make themselves part of "authorizing" whatever "peace keeping" or punitive action is required.

What is the difference between the government practice of China and Iraq? I have never seen or heard that the government practice of a member state was publicly scrutinized or its member privileges brought into question by the United Nations institution itself. Nobody who has been convicted of killing or stealing can sit in any Western parliament. In the United Nations, however, it is quite normal, and the issue is not just individual killings. Votes are being cast by representatives of governments known to have committed mass murders. Some of those ambassadors have probably even been a party to it. Secretary General Boutros Boutros-Ghali is a functionary from a country where the government party has never, I repeat never, had an opposition party. To my knowledge, he is an honorable and able person, but what on earth is his democratic legitimization?

Do we believe that an institution which is supposed to safeguard justice in the world can function if operated by anti-democrats who have no respect for justice at home and trample on the fundamental rights of their own people? Is it democratic, when a country with 100,000 inhabitants, like the Bahamas, has the same voting power as a country with 250 million like the United States? A world which is growing together with great speed no doubt needs institutions which deal with global problems to coordinate necessary actions. I do not believe, however, that the United Nations fits the requirement because of its moral neutrality and ambiguity. It is precisely because of the absence of moral authority and statesmanship in our Western leaders that in order to have somebody else take ultimate responsibility, they hide behind this institution of anonymous people. The same trend can be observed in Europe. European leaders, if they deserve that title, discuss until they are blue in the face what to do about the civil war in former Yugoslavia, but take no significant action. Meanwhile the slaughtering goes on and on. There is no final responsibility and we are heading for disaster.

Latin American Bureaucracy and Corruption

The method of imposing demands which are impossible to meet and then solving the deliberately created problem in return for private remuneration is employed with virtuosity by the Mexican bureaucracy. It is a business worth billions carried on by millions of "public servants"—as frequently today as always. In 1971, when Luis Echeverria was president, there were 700,000 state officials. By 1988, there were almost 4.5 million. One is tempted to conclude that laws and decrees are enacted to enable government bureaucrats to earn suitable extra income. As a business owner in Mexico, I had to contend with this problem every day.

Because of an error by the Customs authorities, five hundred pounds of steel (which I had imported temporarily, without needing to pay duty, for my export business) had not been properly cleared. The duty liability was approximately three hundred dollars. The Finance Ministry imposed a fine of fourteen thousand dollars. The senior official in the same ministry who offered to solve this problem for us as a private citizen, demanded three thousand dollars plus expenses. Anyone who is productive is exposed to constant blackmail and extortion. Greedy bureaucrats, unscrupulous attorneys, and corrupt judges work hand in hand. The result is an apartheid system in which the administrative clique in every social sector lines its own pockets at the expense of the rest of the population. It was not until I came to Mexico that I learned the meaning of legal theft. The English cybernetics expert, Stafford Beer, concluded in 1985 that the Mexican government could perform all its tasks with one-quarter of its state employees. In his view, the bureaucracy looks after its own interests instead of bringing the country's problems any nearer to a solution. I share his opinion and know that no Mexican government "effort" will go anywhere unless the bureaucracy is drastically reduced and corruption on the top level ferociously attacked.

Raul Alfonsin, the former president of bankrupt Argentina, had the brilliant idea of moving the government from Buenos Aires to Viedma in Patagonia in the far south of the country. He expected to cut the bureaucratic apparatus by half through this measure. He imagined that those state employees who, in addition to their civil service job, pursued other lucrative activities in office hours, would prefer to stay in the pleasant area of Buenos Aires rather than settle in the more hostile climate of

Patagonia. Alfonsin thought that the cost of relocation would rapidly be offset by the enormous saving in staff costs. The failure of this project can no doubt be attributed to resistance by his own "public servants."

While school teachers in the Brazilian state of Alagoas earn less than the monthly minimum salary of sixty dollars, this impoverished state in the north of the country paid a dozen bureaucrats salaries of six thousand dollars per month. When he took office in 1987 as the governor of Pernambuco, Miguel Arraes concluded that he needed only 30 percent of his public servants. He, like all new governors, finds it difficult to determine the exact number of personnel at the beginning of his term of office. There are fewer desks than public servants. An army of "phantoms" (or "aviators," as they are called in Mexico) either appear only on payday or hang a jacket over their chair in the morning and leave a pair of glasses on a desk which they collect again in the afternoon.

Government Tax Fraud

A lot of praise has been heaped on Carlos Salinas de Gotari, president of Mexico since 1988. Some say that he is leading Mexico into a new era. We know now that that is not true, because the corruption of the government party, the PRI, which he was heading, continued unabated. Elections continued to be rigged, judges continued to take money instead of administering justice, and I was being blackmailed by government auditors, as usual. The police remained a threat to the safety of the inhabitants of Mexico City, and the ordinary person may have squeezed by but had little hope of improving his lot. It will take more than economic measures to usher in a new era. Instead of lecturing and castigating Haiti for lack of democracy, it would have been more appropriate for the Mexican president, as well as for quite a number of other presidents, to first clean up their own house and build confidence of the people in their own institutions.

Immediately after taking office, Jose Lopez Portillo, president from 1976 until 1982, ordered the director of the Bank of Agriculture, Everardo Espino, to administer his Caja chica, the petty cash account of the president of the Republic. The money was used to bribe publishers and journalists, to finance election campaigns of the ruling party, to pay government bureaucrats gratuities, and to subsidize state-owned companies. Members of the opposition parties, who are part of the system, were also included in the money distribution.

Naturally, this fund was fed with taxpayers' money. That is what irks me most about it—the impunity with which this gang disposes of public funds for their own benefit. The finance ministry supervised the operation, and an audit company audited the expenses—not, of course, with respect to their legality, but only with regards to proper receipts. From 1 January 1977 until 30 September 1979 the equivalent of $10 billion was spent. If you look at the list of the journalists who benefited from this money distribution system, you will not be surprised anymore why the Mexican press for many years never seriously said anything about government corruption, with the result that it continued unabated under every president.

With what authority and on what basis of moral principle does the Mexican government impose taxes and threaten everybody with prison in case of non-compliance? Laws are passed by a Congress which is party to the corruption by not doing anything about it, enforced by a judiciary which is riddled with self-seeking thieves, and implemented by an executive branch which goes after everybody else in the country except themselves and their favored associates. Can that be considered to be moral and, if it is immoral, can it be democratic? Is it right because the formality of a democratic process has been observed and a vote was taken? By no means. It may be legal but not legitimate. What we see is a perversion of democracy presented as the real thing. The enchanting Mexican people deserve something better.

Americans deserve something better as well. The federal government's annual overhead cost is $270 billion, according to an estimate of Congressman Lamar Smith of Texas. A political analyst, Martin L. Gross, suggests that it could be cut by 25 percent, which would bring down the budget deficit by $68 billion annually. In his bestselling book *The Government Racket*,

Gross specifies forty-nine projects to cut costs by \$277 billion per annum. My sister Sibylle, an American citizen, has written President Clinton and asked him to take these suggestions seriously, since he had asked several times for specific and precise suggestions to cut the budget deficit more. Gross is of the opinion that the Bureau of Indian Affairs, for example, is superfluous and should be closed down for an annual savings of \$5 billion. Since I heard a well-known Indian leader, Russell Means, propose exactly the same thing, Gross, with all his other ideas, immediately became credible to me. He further points out that at the turn of the century, when there were five million farms, the Department of Agriculture had three thousand employees. By 1992, there were only about two million farms, but the payroll of the department had swollen to sixty thousand employees. This explains why since 1940 the American population grew by 90 percent while government grew by 5,400 percent. Why subsidize honey and wool production, he asks, especially when the annual \$267 million have to be borrowed or others have to pay higher taxes for it? Even though his list does not cover the totality of government waste, it is abundant proof of government excess and the self-seeking immorality of those politicians who are constantly attempting to justify imposing ever higher taxes. My blood boils when looking at the impunity of those in all countries who continue to raise and waste taxes and the lack of judgment exhibited by those who destroy themselves by empowering such a bunch of incompetents. If tax-paying companies like IBM, General Motors, Boeing, Sears, Volkswagen, Siemens, and so many others have to reorganize their operations and dismiss hundreds of thousands of people to be able to stay in business, why can't government do the same instead of picking the pockets of the taxpayer? There are three reasons for it: selfishness, wrong philosophy of the purpose of government, and management incompetence. The determination of some Republicans to weed out government waste and return government to financial sanity is not only important for America, but should set a trend for the rest of the world.

The political and philosophical reasoning for the rule of bureaucrats without souls is different in the various parts of the world. However, whether under democratic or totalitarian cloak, it is always explained as to serve the needs of the people. The heart of the matter of this worldwide conspiracy against humanity, though, is the power exercised by persons who are not concerned with the welfare of others or with justice, but who are dedicated above all to their own self-interest. The more that people of this kind occupy positions in government, the less that justice will prevail.

The Soviet Failure

The Socialist states are breaking down, but the functionaries continue to govern. Boris Yeltsin believes that the reason that Perestroika had not gotten anywhere and that the lot of ordinary people got worse instead of better, lies in the fact that Gorbachev for all those years did not touch the party bureaucracy and did not deal with the system of privileges. "Naturally times have changed," Yeltsin says, "but the essence of the system has remained the same." Precondition for being successful in a bureaucratic career, he explains, is to be an appeaser and take the road where there is the least resistance. "Obsequiousness and obedience are rewarded in turn by privilege: special hospitals, special vacation retreats, the excellent Central Committee canteen, the equally excellent service for home delivery of groceries and other goods, the Kremlin telephone system, the free transportation. The higher you climb up the professional ladder, the more comforts surround you and the harder and more painful it is to lose them. Therefore the more obedient and dependable you become."[1]

Gorbachev himself had no intention of dealing with the question of leadership's privileges. "On the contrary," said Yeltsin, "instead of renouncing all those completely useless, though pleasant customary perquisites, he built a new house for himself on the Lenin Hills and a new dacha outside Moscow; he had his dacha at Pitsunda rebuilt and then an ultramodern one put up at Thorosin in the Crimea. Finally, to cap it all, at the Congress of People's Deputies he announced with pathos that he has no personal dacha."[2]

Gorbachev did not change the fundamentals in the Soviet Union. Why? Because of his character. He is part of the corruption. He likes to live well in comfort and luxury. "In this he is helped by his wife," describes Yeltsin. "She, unfortunately, is unaware of how keenly and jealously millions of people followed her appearances in the media. She wants to be on view, to play a noticeable part in the life of the country. No doubt in a rich, prosperous, contented society that would be accepted as natural and normal—but not in our country, at least not at this time."[3]

Unfortunately by now the integrity of Yeltsin himself has to be doubted, and I suspect him to be the same Communist as always. Years after the dissolution of the Soviet Union, the privilege system stays intact in Russia. After all, the majority of the members of Parliament are Communists or ex-Communists. The intention to establish a market economy does not lead automatically to the abdication of selfishness, and the Western businessmen who go there probably have no message for changing this attitude.

Development Incorporated

Development Incorporated is the name applied by the journalist and author Graham Hancock in his book *The Lords of Poverty* to the innumerous government and multinational organizations, whose task it is to transfer the economic and financial aid from the industrialized countries to the countries of the Third World. Overpaid bureaucrats could not earn such princely salaries in industry or in government service of their own countries. Their primary interest and focus of their efforts is the enhancement of their own sense of self-importance and their personal well-being. Mismanagement of projects worth billions of dollars is the result.

After nearly fifty years of development aid, the misery of the broad masses in Africa, Latin America, and Asia, which in many cases I know in detail, has not decreased but has increased compared to the state of affairs before it was introduced. This, of course, does not apply to the privileged members of the biggest international bureaucracy, "the aristocracy of mercy," as Hancock calls them, or to the nightclubs, cabarets, restaurants, etc., in the Western metropolis, where these bureaucrats live.

The United Nations employs an army of fifty thousand people. On the political side, you have member countries, which in their majority are undemocratic and whose leaders should be listed as professional thieves and gangsters, who managed to take over government by one way or the other including pure force. On the administrative side you have a waste and corruption of incredible proportions.

Sixty billion dollars is being spent every year—most of it for the staff salaries and related costs. In New York, Rome, Paris, or Geneva—and by no means Kairo, La Paz, or New Delhi—thousands and thousands of bureaucrats sit in their comfortable offices and plan for others, with the money of others, without any effective accountability. They should at least be required to report to the taxpayers and parliaments of the donor nations in the same detailed way that any corporation has to account to its shareholders. Only a small part of those funds reach their intended destination in the developing world, and even when they do, the value of a great many of the projects are questionable. "Perversion of the act of human generosity," is the definition Bob Geldorf used for development aid.

More than two-thirds of the ten thousand functionaries of the Food and Agriculture Organization (FAO) normally sit behind their desks in Rome. "There are 750 of them," describes Hancock, "whose pensionable renumeration ranges from $70,000 to 120,000 a year—these include eleven Assistant Directors General, thirty-one Senior Directors, 125 Directors, 362 Senior Officers and 221 First Officers. The Rector of the United Nations University is paid three times as much as the Norwegian Prime Minister."[4]

It is probably safe to assume that the framework for the responsibilities of these people can be compared to those of the admiral of the Kansas Navy. Director General Edouard Saouma, who serves his third six years term is worth $813.276 net and likes to be addressed "Your Excellency." His salary rivals that of the president of the United States. "One of these men," continues Hancock, referring to the growing number of personnel in the "supergrade" bracket, "an Under-Secretary General, recently retired with a golden handshake of almost half a million dollars plus an annual pension of $50,000. Shortly thereafter the UN rehired him as a consultant at a fee of 125,000 a year."[5]

Saouma and all UNO employees, whether high or low, receive generous fringe benefits, allowances for housing and moving, schools for children, and so forth. Additionally, the excursions into developing countries have to be considered. These provide the opportunity to generate more income through generous daily expense allowances, which are only partially spent. The UNO mother company in New York budgets annually $100 million for travelling expenses. These travels are not necessarily undertaken into project areas. The majority consists of seminars, conferences, visits to representatives of donor nations, and similar exhausting exercises.

Some members of the European Parliament show the same virtuosity in transforming the daily expense allowance into personal gain. They spend the night on the couches in their offices and pocket the pay for the hotel. In order to avoid unpleasant surprises, the floors of their offices are not patrolled by security guards during the night. That way no one notices that the companion of the evening is not necessarily wife or husband.

Eighty percent of the annual UNESCO budget of $185 million are normally spent in Paris, where headquarters are located. This is a great boom for the profitability of restaurants and nightclubs.

Whoever thinks that royal payment means compensation for extraordinary qualification, errs. "There is nothing to indicate that systematic efforts are being made either to require a high level of staff qualifications or to train professional staff for specific tasks they will be called upon to perform. On the contrary, the laxness that prevails in this matter would seem to put a premium on mediocrity,"[6] concludes Maurice Bertrand, a senior member of the United Nations Joint Inspection Unit. "Thus, at every level of the multilateral agencies, maladjusted, inadequate, incompetent individuals are to be found clinging tenaciously to highly paid jobs, timidly and indifferently performing their functions and, in the process, betraying the world's poor in whose name they have been appointed,"[7] concludes Hancock.

There are fifty-seven assistant secretaries general and under-secretaries general in the New York headquarters alone. But apparently they and their colleagues are so overworked, that the United Nations, in addition to their staff of 50,000, send thousands of so-called experts (150,000 of them employed each year) into the Third World for counselling. World Bank, OECD, and national development institutions do the same. Each expert, the majority of whom are recruited from the industrialized nations, costs between $100,000 and 150,000 per year. That amounts to a total of between $15 billion to $22 billion.

World Bank and International Monetary Fund (IMF) apply the same generous principle: highly paid functionaries leave periodically from Washington to the countries in need of help, meet with government representatives, decree structural adjustments, and finance projects of doubtful value according to ever-changing criteria. On the one side of the table, there is the overpaid development experts, and on the other side, the representatives of government bureaucracies, very often nothing else but gangsters in government cloth who are only interested in their own commissions. Therefore, a lot of structural adjustments of the IMF are really irrelevant, even though they sound good and reasonable. The real problem preventing progress in every developing country is not addressing the bloated and corrupt government bureaucracy. In November 1992, the Executive Board of the World Bank discussed an internal report according to which 37.5 percent of all projects completed by the end of 1991 were failures. An earlier report of February 1992 evaluated 359 completed projects with a total investment volume of $43 billion. Thirty-six percent of those projects had already failed when the funding was completed, and half of the remaining 230 projects would never be viable.

I want to cite one example of the innumerable facts Hancock cites—a typical project, not an exception. The actor in this case was the European Community, which in 1982 had commissioned a construction company from Milan, Italy, to build a road from Mogadischu, the capital of Somalia, to the port city of Kismaoyo. The road was completed in 1983 and has been unusable since 1988 because of the sloppy work provided by the Italian construction company. Somalia is supposed to repay the $100 million loan plus interest provided by the European Community. Payments were scheduled until the year 2023. Naturally there will be no more payment—money completely wasted.

It would have been better to ask the Chilean construction company to do the job, which during the presidency of General Pinochet did an excellent job building the double lane road from Santiago to San Antonio. But the perversity of Western development aid prescribes that any given project must benefit the donor's economy. This kind of "loving your neighbor" was described by former U.S. President Richard Nixon: "The main purpose of our aid is not to help other nations but to help ourselves."

Hancock reaches the conclusion that development aid by nature is bad and cannot be reformed. He insists that it should be abolished because, as he says:

> To continue with the charade seems to me absurd. Garnered and justified in the name of the destitute and the vulnerable, aid's main function in the past half-century has been to create and then entrench a powerful new class of rich and privileged people. In that notorious club of parasites and hangers-on made up of the United Nations, the World Bank and the bilateral agencies. It is aid—and nothing else—that provided hundreds of thousands of "jobs for the boys" and that has permitted record-breaking standards to be set in self-serving behaviour, arrogance, paternalism, moral cowardice and mendacity. At the same time, in the developing countries, aid has perpetuated the rule of incompetent and venal men, whose leadership would otherwise be utterly non-viable. It has allowed governments, characterised by historic ignorance, avarice, and irresponsibility to thrive. Last but not least, it has condoned—and in some cases facilitated—the most consistent and grievous abuses of human rights that have occurred anywhere in the world since the dark ages.[8]

I agree with Hancock. His book should serve for every parliament of donor countries as a base for discussion and decision. Indeed, where are the results of decades of developmental aid? What we see is a growing misery of the masses in countries heavily indebted—like in the Soviet Union after decades of mismanagement by another set of bureaucrats—but with ruling elites who have stolen enough to lead a comfortable life. Developmental aid as practiced by Western governments is a Socialist misconstruction.

I suggest that the United Nations, the World Bank, and all government-related national and international development organizations be dissolved. With the billions saved each year, one could double the salaries of teachers in the developing countries and cancel their debt on the condition that the bureaucracy be reduced at least by half. In addition to this, protectionist trade barriers of industrialized countries must be abolished. We would get what we say we have: a free market society. Some of the developing countries could take off like a rocket. Most of the $1.2 trillion debt of Eastern Europe and the developing world will never be paid back anyway.

St. Augustine and the Bureaucracy

When he was navy secretary, John Lehman described the Pentagon bureaucracy as a "socialist culture." He was also highlighting the central feature of the Marxist economic and social theory which is used to justify envious and power-hungry bureaucrats to obtain posts with a high salary and the possibility of controlling others whom they exploit. Marx considered the capitalists' possession of the means of production as the root of all evil. Quite apart from the fact that this analysis is incorrect, it would certainly be outmoded today. In any case, the exploitation of man by man is practiced all over the world by egotistic and noncaring bureaucracies. The only difference between individual countries resides in the margin of freedom which remains for the individual. Totalitarian regimes stand at one extreme of the scale. In the Soviet Union, the nomenclature has treated men like cattle and looked upon them as their own property. However, this approach in itself does not touch on the heart of the matter but only the outer surface of the evil, as I have pointed out elsewhere.

St. Augustine asked:

> How then do empires differ from great band of robbers
> if they know no justice? Bands of robbers are no different
> from empires. A band of robbers is a horde of men who
> gang together under the command of a leader to share the
> booty on an agreed scale. If this evil structure spreads
> through the addition of dissolute individuals to such an
> extent that it takes over localities, sets up dependencies,
> conquers towns and submits peoples to its will, it assumes
> the name of state. Its greed does not disappear but it
> gains immunity from punishment.[9]

The answer once given by a captured sea pirate to Alexander
the Great was both appropriate and true. When the king asked
this man why he was making the sea so unsafe, he answered
with bold defiance: "And why are you making the earth so
unsafe? Of course because I have a small vessel, I am called a
robber. You have a big fleet and are called 'emperor'."[10]

The Democratic Fraud

Honesty is a necessary precondition for democracy to function. It is dishonest to initiate and pass legislation using issues
for purely political purposes without being interested primarily
in the issue. Issues are being used to gain an advantage on
political opponents. Nothing is being solved, interest is only
pretended. Where there is such dishonesty in the political process, democracy is undermined. In the minds of innumerable
people, especially of those who do not vote anymore, this kind
of dishonesty, apparent especially during election time, is identified as politics and taken as a disgusting fact of life.

Democratic leaders furthermore have associated with criminal and totalitarian regimes and their representatives, either
nationally or internationally, for personal or national advantages. This destroys the very foundations on which democracy is
built and can only be called anti-democratic. J.F. Kennedy's use
of his mistress to get Mafia boss Sam Giancana to help him win
the West Virginia primary, means that the leader of the strongest Western democracy was participating in the destruction of
democratic substance. Little can make our Western fraud clearer.

Furthermore, the collaboration of democratic nations and their leaders with totalitarian rulers is the worst violation of human rights. All Western countries, with total disregard of the unhappy people within Iraq, played up to Saddam Hussein, wanting him as a client or an ally, and created this dangerous monster. We may rightfully condemn the torture of individual people in different countries by their governments and lecture them on human rights, but our appeasement of the Hitlers, Stalins, Gorbachevs, Husseins, and Assads is much worse and causes infinitely more suffering. I say it is undemocratic. It is national self-seeking based on the wrong concept of national interest.

The passionate defense of the democratic process by Sen. Joseph Biden at the end of the Thomas Hearings in the Senate Judiciary Committee, in face of widespread dismay about the procedure, was besides the point. I agree with his statement that democracy is an imperfect instrument of government, but only insofar as it relates to our conception and practice of democracy. He said, like others did before him, that nobody has come up with something better. Well, I am coming up right here on these pages not only with something better, but with a concept of how government is meant to be. It does not matter, as Biden stressed, that Senate procedures have existed and served their purpose for more than two hundred years. The point is that today the democratic contents of these procedures are under attack from undemocratic forces who, like Joseph Goebbels and his Nazi gang, use the democratic armament to destroy democracy from within in order to impose their own intolerant views on everybody. We must therefore not just change the mechanics but the substance to prevent the perversion of the system.

There is, though, a substantial difference between the times of Goebbels, who was a master in manipulating public opinion for political purposes, and now. The difference is television. That somebody like Anita Hill, who alleges something about somebody else after ten years of silence a few days before a crucial vote, and gets a Senate platform to air her pornographic allegations on television for hours and hours without having been scrutinized beforehand on her credibility and character, is bizarre. That the accused, who has been screened by the FBI several times, has an impeccable personal record and has to defend himself against hearsay in front of millions of people without any legal recourse, is incredible. It is a clear demonstration of the subversion of democratic values and institutions which we are witnessing. Unfortunately this is not an isolated incident but a recognizable pattern.

There is a fundamental misconception at the heart of American democracy. The elected person is being sent to Washington to slice off as many federal funds as possible in whatever form for his constituency. Americans in general consider their senator or congressman to be a representative of their personal material interests. He has to attend their wishes or be replaced at the next election. Most people want to get something out of him instead of helping him to listen to the voice of responsibility and find solutions for America and the world. The corruption of democracy is not just an affair of the politicians. It is an affair in which every citizen bears responsibility. Decision making on the basis of opinion polls, instead of conviction about issues, is a major flaw in democracy. It is true that government has to account to the people. But that does not mean that it has to serve the greed of those people. If government representatives do it, it is because of their own greed.

Western politicians believe that they possess the wisdom and the right to teach others about democracy and human rights and to punish those in other cultures who do not agree with their own particular point of view. They fail to see that in our morally degenerate society, the corruption of our democratic institutions and procedures speak louder than their democratic affirmations. The crucifixion of justice by appeasing voter's demands for the benefit of one's reelection is the most devastating democracy-destroying motivation. In spite of the internationalization of our contemporary world, most politicians remain prisoners of small local interests because of their own self-seeking motivations. Former Secretary of Defense Caspar Weinberger pointed out that most of the important decisions of Congress are taken on the basis of causing offense to the smallest possible number of electors and satisfying the largest possible number of interest groups.

A member of the German cabinet once told me that he was the only one in that group who had ever lived outside Germany. The same is true, I am afraid, of most cabinets around the world. The result is provincialism, a narrow outlook on world affairs with a lack of understanding of other people and cultures. Such politicians constantly project their own concepts and traditions on far-away situations and tend to make enemies rather than friends. There are innumerable presidents, prime ministers, and foreign ministers who speak nothing but their own language. While in every other career there are professional requirements to be met by anyone who wants to get into a position of responsibility, there are no such criteria for politicians. The German Parliament used to consist largely of lawyers, government employees, and trade union functionaries who produce a very lopsided approach to issues. There should be more variation related to the composition of society. But above all, nobody should become president or prime minister, who has not lived some years in one or more foreign countries.

From Corrupt to Inspired Democracy

There is a worldwide reaction of the people against their establishments. In some totalitarian states, they went on the streets to bring down their rulers. In the democracies, they boycott the election booth or vote for outsiders hoping for a change. Ronald Reagan, a very popular president, was elected by about 25 percent of the voting population; Clinton got in by only 23.3 percent. People cry for the real thing and don't know what it is. They only know that the worm is in what they have.

The democratic process in our Western democracies has become more and more a battle between self-seeking interest groups, fought out on the backs of the people who have to pay for the circus. Whoever can bring the strongest pressure, wins a given contest. The process is determined by a group of professionals within the party structures, who control nominations and appointments, and you either hop on the bandwagon or get out. The only choice ordinary people have is to vote on what is presented to them or abstain. The outcome of this is "the establishment," a mixture of people in elected office or in administrative dependencies of the government. They consider themselves the legitimate representatives of democracy with the right to administer the people. An attack on them is seen as an attack on democracy. They help each other worldwide, because any breach in the system anywhere could have negative repercussions on them and their ability to control the government apparatus. That explains, in part, the "democratic indignation" about the action of Peru's Fujimori mentioned earlier. I might add that the liberal media, as part of the establishment, attacks anybody around the world who shows independence and refuses to fit into their Socialist pattern.

Of course we need governments and administrations—it would be foolish to say that we can do without them. What is wrong is the motivation of those who make up the establishment. Not all are guilty, however. There is genuine service and a lot of frustration for those who get caught in the web and are unable to cut through it. What is wrong is the attempt to substitute morals with rules and accept selfishness as normal. The consequence is a bloated bureaucracy and financial mismanagement. Selfishness in the democratic process is like sand in a machine: it destroys. It is the self-seeking within the apparatus which leads to self-seeking in international affairs, to the contradictions in our approach, and to an immoral foreign policy. But the self-seeking originates in society, in each person who blindly just wants "to get." We have forgotten that character is more important than rules. Without genuine concern for other people, selfless service of those within and without the establishment, and commitment to a value system, democracy cannot function. Without obedience to God, democracy and society will perish. We proclaim victory in the Cold War because we are blind toward the reality of the present-day political and social trend. Societies emptied of ethics and purpose are being realigned under the rule of similarly minded bureaucrats, who have a firm grip on the national resources and distribute the fruits of the productivity of their citizens among themselves.

In his study of democracy, the German philosopher Karl Jaspers explains that it may lead to the tyranny of the majority or to the rule of lawlessness if the misuse of the resources of democracy destroys the idea which lies at its root. "Democracy is tolerant of all possibilities," writes Jaspers,

> but must itself be able to become intolerant of intolerance. It is opposed to force but must resist force with force. It permits all spiritual, social and political movements, but where those movements through their organization and action turn against the process of democratic reason, the force of the State must itself be able to intervene in response. Democratic politicians and officials, unworthy of democracy, are spun into a web of legal niceties by the intelligence of those individuals who wish to put an end to legality. They cannot free themselves from this web and conceal the fact that they have lost their opportunity by talking and taking frenetic action without in fact doing anything. The idea of democracy is lost in the hands of mere politicians who allow it to fade away in a pseudo-democratic emotionally agitated life.

"Democracy," Jaspers continues, "is an idea which is constantly changing and whose attainment depends on the quality of those who represent it . . . The path towards that idea is constantly marked out by a search for truth in a democratic community."[11]

There is not one government in the world, not the German and not the government of the United States, to name only two, which has an acceptable purpose. Governments are self-seeking and not God-seeking, no matter what they proclaim. The mushrooming bureaucracy, ever-higher taxes, new programs, and the growing debt are expressions of this fact. Governments have trapped their people for their own sake, but people have also let themselves be trapped. That is why the approach to cut the budget deficit, as necessary as that is, falls far short of what is needed and is unlikely to last. The purpose of any government has to be defined anew and then, I am convinced, a multitude of agencies can simply be liquidated. Government reduced to size. Does it need a Secretariat of Education, a Bureau for Indian Affairs, a Secretariat of Commerce?

The path is clear. A new purpose and a change in motives of those who represent and make up democracy is what is necessary: from self-seeking to God-seeking. God-seeking means seeking justice for the world, even if it hurts one's own nation and oneself. Such a change is possible. Then we shall turn a corrupt democracy into an inspired democracy.

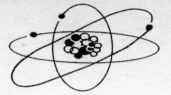

Western Society

The United States of America is the leading country of Western society. There are millions of people around the world who dream of coming to this land of the free, to have a chance to make a good living and experience the fulfillment of the American dream. For me, a typical American always has meant a warm-hearted, generous and optimistic person who is eager to communicate with others—characteristics which I thought were reflected on the government level by the post-World War II Marshall Plan. Through its lifestyle, music, films, political and economic organization, and action, America has had a world-wide influence like no other nation in modern times. It is also the one nation that has freedom as a birthright and as a global mission. The reason for the existence of the nation is not a common ancestry but the concept of and the dedication to liberty.

What we see today, however, is a deeply divided, socially disintegrating, and debt-ridden country, with people who are very unsure of themselves. As parents, my wife Dina and I are deeply concerned over the dangers our children have to face as they grow up. We fear what might be done to their bodies, minds and souls in a society which has no respect for the life and integrity of human beings, but still considers itself the most advanced in human history. Since Stefan and Sabrina speak several languages, we could as well have them grow up and go to school in Europe or Latin America, but those societies offer a similar picture and the same, if not worse, dangers. We have gone through our options in detail and come to the conclusion that it is all of Western society which is in crisis and that we cannot escape the challenge and the task of doing something about it if we love our children and care about others. What has happened to America? Where is Western society heading? What makes us Westerners tick? Who is leading and in which direction? Is anybody leading at all, or are we just drifting?

Once every minute a young person somewhere in the United States tries to commit suicide. Every nineteen minutes, one succeeds. Abortion claims the lives of 1.6 million unborn children each year in America and this has been going on since 22 January 1973, the day on which Harry Blackmun and his colleagues on the U.S. Supreme Court declared abortion legal. In the succeeding twenty years, 30 million human lives have been destroyed in this way. That is more than five times as many as the number of Jews assassinated in the gas chambers by the Nazis. Hitler's program of euthanasia, the destruction of "inferior" life, was harmless in comparison with the mass murder practiced today. In Germany "only" four hundred thousand to five hundred thousand unborn children are sent to their death by their mothers every year. According to a survey by the Alan Guttmacher Institute, only 1 percent of abortions are because of rape or incest. All the others are being performed for convenience in various forms and because of the greed of the doctors involved.

Twelve million children in the United States come from broken marriages. Each year the parents of one million children divorce, thus depriving those children of a family life. Sixteen million children live in households without a father. Two and a half million fathers owe $2.5 billion in child support. A quarter of a million children are born out of wedlock yearly. And if this trend continues, fostered by an insane welfare system, there will be more children born out of wedlock than inside families by the end of the century. A growing number of mothers are schoolgirls. One million children between the ages of six and sixteen are sexually abused each year in America. In a recent survey of the sexual behavior of all teen-agers, it was found that 39.6 percent of ninth graders, 47.6 percent of tenth graders, 57.3

percent of eleventh graders and 71.9 percent of twelfth graders have had sexual intercourse. Four percent have had a sexually transmitted disease. In total, according to the U.S. Department of Health and Human services, three million teen-agers are infected every year with sexually transmitted diseases. A nation-wide survey conducted in 1990 by the Centers of Disease Control shows that 19 percent of U.S. high-school students have had four or more sex partners.

And now we have AIDS. A Harvard University research team predicted in June 1992 that 120 million people will be infected worldwide by the end of the century. According to the World Health Organization, 30 to 40 million of these will be Americans. The 1992 U.S. budget contained $4.4 billion for federal AIDS spending. In 1993 it increased to $4.9 billion. According to Frederick Hellinger of the US Agency for Health Care Policy and Research, total cost will soon rise to $15.2 billion. We shall see astronomical figures by the end of the century. But no money is going to cure the epidemic which is the logical consequence of the perversion of our morals. The few people who get infected by blood transfusion, a dentist, or something similar, are less than 2 percent. The bulk of the infection comes through drug addicts and homosexuals, who, according to a study by the American Psychological Association of 1984, have an average of fifty sex partners a year. The next growing group of individuals at risk are the sexually promiscuous of all ages and preferences.

AIDS is not just a venereal disease, but an epidemic caused by the immorality of a whole society. The only solution is for people to live straight. The country needs political leaders whose political platform includes clarification of this central issue for society instead of promising nonsense like legislation, safe sex education, condoms in schools, etc. Society, after all, has to pay for the promiscuousness which is so prevalent. It will cost $102,000 for medical care for each AIDS-infected person, according to Hellinger. AIDS is an easy illness to eliminate. Just stop pairing like dogs and use sex only for the purpose for which God has created—an expression of love in marriage and for procreation. Instead, people go on the streets and demonstrate government support for perverted lifestyles.

In essence, the perverts are asking that others pay the bill for the consequences of their uncontrolled lust. It is like a motorcyclist smashing into one shop window after another, causing damage each time, but refusing to stop because he considers it "his right," and then demanding others to pay for the damage. Is the taxpayer supposed to pick up the tab for people who refuse to control themselves? Homosexuality is wrong, not just because it is having intercourse with a member of the same sex, but because a person does not have the right to unlimited sex for pleasure with whomever he or she chooses without responsibility. A society which divides people into "heterosexuals" and "homosexuals" and makes no moral distinctions is fatally sick. I do not want to be classified like that.

Ten million Americans are alcoholics and another eight million have drinking problems. This results in unhappy families, reduced performance at work, and rising medical costs—the related costs are estimated at $117 billion annually.

A study revealed at the end of the eighties that more than half of America's high-school students cannot properly read and write. But, these same students know about the use of condoms, which are distributed by educators who seduce young people to evil habits. Similarly Nazi educators seduced German youth to other evils. "Good pay and little work" summarizes the aspirations of these young flag bearers of future democracy. Education must be ethical and global or it does not deserve the name education.

Some years ago I was driving south on the highway from the Frankfurt airport. A car in front of me had a sticker on its rear window which read, "I love pleasure and I want it now." At the same time a voice crooned out of my car radio: "There is no sin in the eleventh commandment. . . . Don't try to tell me, that what we are doing is sinful because love is life. Your eyes are so tender and your mouth is so red . . . If we go to heaven we will not be able to kiss, and if we go to hell there will be nothing to drink. So let us enjoy life while we can."

The quality of human society is determined by the quality of life of the people who together constitute that society. The quality of life is not an economic parameter, but is determined by the content each individual gives to his life and by the goals and objectives he sets for himself.

The more that men live for their own pleasure and see work only as a means to attain that end, the lower will be the quality of the society constituted by such men. Obviously, the more people show the qualities that we see in America's founding fathers, the more valuable will be a society composed of such people. What would a Christian society look like in which Christians did not only preach but actually followed the teachings of Jesus? Quality is not a question of being right but of living beyond oneself. The quality of our free society is being largely reduced to the search for pleasure that is reflected in the sticker and song I quoted earlier referring to what is no longer a mere passing fancy, but the substance of many men's and women's lives. People whose lives have no content and who live only for their daily pleasure consider that lifestyle to be their democratic right.

There is a growing pressure to remove all criteria of character and morality from our educational systems. Politicians treat the crisis in education worldwide as a matter of lack of funds. But no money is going to resolve the mess. Instead of teaching children how to live with others in our society, so as to achieve the fruits of true knowledge, they are taught "critical disobedience." "How can children defend themselves against their parents?" is the question put into the coursebook for religious education of ten to fifteen year olds in Germany entitled *Obedience and Maturity in the Family*. This book gives detailed advice on ways in which children can escape from the troublesome rules laid down by their parents. The green party in Germany calls for the right for school children to strike. A judge in Florida ruled that an eleven-year-old boy may divorce his parents. The German book entitled *Religion today for young people aged between 16 and 18* contains the following observations: "The changes must reach right down to the smallest cell in society, the traditional family which must be transformed into a large family with broader sexual links. . . . Ultimately there must no longer be any private ownership of washing machines, women and children." When concepts of class warfare, the intellectual advancing guard of totalitarianism, are carried by political illiterates into school and family, neglect of the family is elevated in the school and promoted by "social" legislation. In 1975 the Educational Policy Commission of the Social Democratic party in Germany already described the family as old-fashioned and sexual encounters with various others as desirable. This thought pattern is then reflected in school books and innocent children are exposed to indoctrination which destroys both family and society. The presentation of homosexuality as a legitimate lifestyle is only a part of it. Will American high schools send illiterate sex maniacs into a university system, which is the finest in the world? The United Nations women's conference in Beijing in September 1995 promoted the same trend, promoting so-called children's rights. Ultimately the aim is to destroy the authority of parents and, therewith, the family. The "rights" of the children are pitched against the authority of the parents. Most concepts regarding human rights promoted by the United Nations are divisive. Why should any Western nation take any cue regarding our family life from a faceless and godless organization?

According to the Chicago University professor, Allan Bloom, "the lack of education simply results in students seeking for enlightenment wherever it is readily available, without being able to distinguish between the sublime and trash, insight and propaganda."[1] He describes how at Cornell University, the faculty gave in to a student mob which threatened violence, and met absurd demands which led to the curriculum being reduced to the level of the laziest and least gifted. He compares the cowardliness of that university board which lacked the courage to defend its own integrity with the cowardly professors of the 1930s in Heidelberg, Germany, who gave in to Nazi pressure. But Bloom highlights one fundamental difference: By expressing opposition the Germans would have risked their own lives, but the Americans faced no risk at all. However, in both cases the result is the same. An evil spirit which endangers human dignity wins the day and eats away at the fabric of our society.

The Communists and Nazis conducted, and are still conducting in some parts of the world, a resolute war against any religious influence on society, because a higher morality stands in the way of the exercise of their own power. But if God cannot be completely eliminated, as experience proved, he must at the very least be displaced into the sphere of private life. The Russian Orthodox Church was not allowed to take issue with the state or society, and church leaders had to present their teachings in accordance with Communist philosophy. We had precisely the same in Nazi Germany. A bishop with the name of Mueller was the head of the so-called German Christians, who subordinated Christian teachings to Nazi requirements.

Western Socialist destroyers of society, who call themselves liberals in some countries, are following exactly the same prescription. God and his influence must be removed from school and society. Anyone who so wishes can sing hymns at home or worship in church, but no Christian morality is allowed where it matters. This of course has nothing to do with religion as such, but with morality. The discussion in America as to whether prayers are permissible in schools, whether Christmas carols could be sung in public, and whether the Christmas tree should not be called a holiday tree has its root in the same endeavor to create a system of education and a society which knows no values but appeals only to the intellect, to the exclusion of character, ethics and religion. At the same time, standards are lowered and achievement condemned as elitist. The concept of separation of church and state, which is not mentioned in the American constitution, is taken as a pretext to evade those uncomfortable moral precepts of Christianity. As a matter of fact, this view, put into practice today and forced upon society by judges who have lost the connection to the roots of justice, is a misconception.

Theater, television, and movies continually promote the same lifestyle exhibited by *Penthouse*, *Playboy*, and similar magazines. "Let's turn the theater into a brothel," announced Peter Zadek, the director of the Hamburg State Theater, and who went on to stage "Lulu," a second-rate pornographic work which he advertised with placards showing the unclothed lower part of a woman's body in front of the face of a gnome. A previous production,

"Andi," was on the same cultural level. Zadek's advertising poster showed the naked backside of the leading actor. The American pornographic journals which I mentioned earlier are financed by companies seeking to increase their turnover and profits by advertisements which appear between the naked bodies of women. In Germany it is the taxpayer who is funding the filth and nonsense on the stage, yet has no say in what is being shown. If someone objects, he is immediately accused of trying to introduce censorship. All German theaters are subsidized. Zadek not only earned $135,000 a year, he was also given $40,000 extra from the cultural budget of the Hamburg Senate for each production, including both "Lulu" and "Andi."

In the U.S., Robert and Linda Richter, from the Center for Media and Public Affairs, and Prof. Stanley Rothman, director of the Center for the Study of Social and Political Change at Smith College, point out that 75 percent of TV's elite consider themselves politically to be left of center and most of them want to move society towards their views and not just entertain people. Sixty-five percent believe that the structure of U.S. society needs to be reformed. Eighty percent see nothing wrong with homosexual relationships, and an overwhelming majority reject traditional restrictions on extramarital sex and abortion. These restrictions are being presented as barriers to human fulfillment and gay rights are championed.

According to the American Family Association, the three major networks in 1991 displayed ten thousand sexual incidents during prime time. By the time a child leaves elementary school, the child has seen eight thousand TV murders according to estimates by a task force of the American Psychological Association. Additionally, children see approximately twenty thousand commercials a year offering immediate gratification. So what they learn to want is immediate gratification and others must deliver the goods. "Fascination with evil" is the description Michael Medved uses in his comprehensive analysis of the American film industry in his book *Hollywood vs. America*. The filth which is being carried into our living rooms, is the responsibility of the producers, the networks, and the actors, as well. Why don't the actors refuse to take part in it? Why do they do it? Is it for the glamour, the money, or because of their own lifestyle? Are there no actors to speak up and attempt to clean out the mud which engulfs their profession? Is there only Michael Medved who has the guts to call a spade a spade?

Is it a question of different lifestyles, which we discuss and work out on our road to a richer and more satisfying society? Do women need more rights, business more control, teenagers more condoms, government more money? Is it up to the nine judges in the Supreme Court and their colleagues around the world to determine what we may and may not do? Are the generous programs of Congress, funded, with other people's money, going to turn the tide? Or will it be the Ross Perots, the Colin Powells, or someone like them who will lead the people out of the mess?

I believe that we have sunk already so deep into our morass, that it will be very difficult to get out, let alone clean it up. Democratic society is in the middle of a crisis which is deepening as time passes. This mess is threatening our very existence, much more than the nuclear arsenal of the Soviet Union ever did. Our fragmented society has activists in each segment who are for or against something. Everybody is being labelled. You are conservative or liberal, moderate Right or new Left, progressive or reactionary, prochoice or prolife, Baptist or Catholic, radical Religious Right or Civil Rights, and once you are put into such a box, certain attitudes and views are attributed to you. That permits avoiding any possible moral evaluation and playing political games with the boxes instead. Everything becomes relative and is on the same footing. This way, a homosexual is not a pervert but rather a person with a different lifestyle that in a tolerant and democratic society has to be respected. Next, under disguise of education, books promoting homosexual behavior like *Heather Has Two Mommies* or *Daddy's Roommate*, are being introduced into the school system in order to destroy the moral foundation of defenseless children.

As politicians declare national problems to be mainly of economic and financial nature, they come up with a variety of plans and programs—some have merit, and some don't. Those with merit will, if implemented, slow our downslide but none of them will essentially change the trend. I have seen no political or spiritual leader around the world—except Alan Keyes—who has addressed head-on the central issue in the world of today, which of course is not economic but only has economic repercussions. We are sinking into a moral abyss with the consequence of a disintegrating society and the danger of self-destruction. The advancing technologies and the demise of the Soviets only hide the fact. The biggest need of individuals and humanity today is the necessity for integration, for being at peace with oneself, one's country, and with humanity. There is a great difference between forcing people and nations into faceless bureaucratic structures and nations growing with their traditions and customs into harmonious alliances on the basis of the same values and objectives.

One reason for the Americans' difficulty to perceive reality is the underlying assumption that the organization of the country and the government is okay and only needs improving. Americans are justly proud of their democratic tradition and institutions and of being the advancing guard for freedom around the world. It is difficult, therefore, for them to understand that their whole system is rotten and has to be renewed. It is easier for me because personal experience with the Nazis makes me look very hard at what any government does and under what pretext.

The American way of life has been hijacked and distorted by homosexuals, abortionists, envious, godless judges and corrupt lawmakers—and also by comfortable and indifferent people. Abortion, homosexuality, divorce, the AIDS epidemic, widespread drug use, violence, out-of-wedlock children in the millions, alcoholism, mushrooming national debt, and rampant dishonesty in universities, in financial institutions, and in government are being treated as individual issues but can never be cured on a separate basis. They are not, in reality, independent problems, but symptoms of a deadly illness of world society, and the cause must be treated to achieve a cure. America, having been the vanguard society since its founding as a nation, has to cure the illness for all humanity. At the base of the demise of society is the unbridled selfishness of men and women who put their own demands before anything else. They follow their greed and their lust with total disregard for the consequences. Each one of us can take up the battle, attacking one's own selfishness. Start with the acts most obvious to even yourself. I started with washing dishes at home instead of leaving it to my mother and sister. There is no other way to cure the problem except by starting with oneself. If you point your finger at your neighbor there are three pointing back at you.

My wife is a true homemaker, the backbone of our family. It would never occur to Dina to go to bed in the evening, even if she scarcely can keep her eyes open, without having offered me dinner. I love her for it, not because of the fantastic food she always puts in front of me, but because of her commitment which is behind that act. And of course, I don't demand it. The other day our Doberman got seriously ill and disappeared. Dina was very worried, walked around the house, then took the car to search for the dog, which eventually came back scarcely able to move. Dina dropped everything and took her to the veterinarian. It was, I thought, a rather strange behavior for a person, who says she doesn't like dogs and complains so often that she always has to clean up the mess the dog causes in the house. So why is it that she is beside herself, when suddenly something threatens the life of the same dog? The answer is simple, the dog is the apple of Stefan's eye. She knows that her son, Stefan, would be grief stricken if something serious would happen to Aptik, his dog. This shows the soul of a mother, who would give her life for the well-being of her children without even thinking about it.

The arguments of the activists for women's rights don't impress me very much. The rejection of self and God is at the heart of their philosophy. Most of the feminists, I suspect, have never tried to build a family. Some consider marriage slavery. This is because they go out "to get" and not "to give" even though they might dedicate themselves to health care or other noble causes. Americans tend to get absorbed with side issues like "harassment at the workplace," "abuse of children," "discrimination of so and so," etc. Of course harassment of whomever by whomever is wrong, but in recent years we tend to blow these things out of proportion. When we lose the center of our lives and focus on side issues, we don't cure anything but only invent new rules.

I am not saying that the woman belongs in the kitchen, even though some NOW (National Organization for Women) activists may so accuse me. And let it be known I'm not against being in the kitchen myself. Dina and I founded a travel agency in Mexico several years ago. Dina ran the agency for many years. One of the principal reasons for this was that I wanted Dina to have her complete independence from me, to be on equal footing. She was running the agency, I was managing our factory.

Then she encountered a conflict between the business and her concept of responsibility for our growing children. She had to decide, since she couldn't do the two things adequately at the same time: be in business or be at the side of her children when they needed her. There was no hesitation whatsoever, the children came first. Eventually we sold the agency after losing a lot of money. There is a woman I adore. She knows her God-given calling and has her priorities as a woman and a mother. A society which loses this central ingredient and replaces it with the emptiness of a feminist's ambition is doomed to perish.

A collection of individuals seeking their own goals without a common purpose beyond themselves adds up to a society without a purpose. A society without purpose cannot last. But it has to be the right purpose. The French Revolution had the wrong purpose; it developed the idea of society as the carrier of destiny linked with faith in a vocation. This was then reshaped by Karl Marx into his concept of a classless society as the fulfillment of human history, and then adopted by Adolf Hitler, who claimed that German society in the form of the people's community under his leadership had been given by providence a special role in the world.

The French Revolution set the seal on the social breach between theory and practice. They introduced the double-talk which dominates politics today. What did their liberty, equality, and brotherhood look like? The murderers who lynched the commander of the Bastille on 14 July 1789 have become national heroes who are still celebrated today. The assassination of the king was followed a century later by the murder of the Czar.

The practice of beheading opponents in massive numbers was further developed on a grand scale in the German gas chambers, Soviet gulags, Chinese labor camps, and Cuban torture prisons. Millions of young Europeans were sacrificed on the Altar of the Fatherland, which was followed by other altars. Bishop Talleyrand, who was the precursor of Bishop Mueller of the German Reich, and Archbishop Tutu each prostituted Christianity and its vocabulary to serve a political interest in the power struggle of their times. The "revolutionary court" became a "people's court" in Nazi Germany. The terror of the Jacobins as an instrument for the exercise of power was followed by the terror of the Gestapo, the KGB, the Stasi, and similar organizations. The self-seeking of the dispossessed rulers was replaced by the corruption of the new rulers.

The fight against the church and church closures in France marked the beginning of the revolt of state and society against God. The erection of an altar to the god of reason in front of Notre Dame Cathedral, and the replacement of church services by ceremonies in honor of the martyrs of the revolution in other temples, turned the concept of a society based on liberty, equality, and fraternity into a farce. The prophets of that high ideal thought only of their own equality and not of others. They lacked the strength of character to implement the ideal which they proclaimed—precisely what a growing number of people in Western countries feel about their democratic spokesmen today.

As is the case now, the European leaders and intellectuals at the time of Robespierre could only see what was happening before their very eyes on the political scene. Some were for and some were against what they saw. Some welcomed the end of the absolute monarchy, and others deplored it—but all failed to see the warning signs of a spiritual storm. In the same way, most people fail to see the warning signs today. No matter how confused the course of politics may have been in the two centuries following the events and leading up to the present, the spiritual points were set in the wrong direction. That is why I believe that it is naive to hail the "victory" of the Cold War as a turning point in human history. The temporary downfall of Gorbachev and the Soviet Empire has certainly brought profound changes and great opportunities for many. But the underlying trends of what moves society have not changed at all. On the contrary, there is an acceleration towards catastrophe because Western people and their leaders are blind to reality.

Totalitarian regimes, including those in Islamic countries, satisfy up to a certain point, the human longing for purpose and oneness of man, society, and the world. Democracy so far has utterly failed to even recognize the issue. Contrary to the French Revolution, the United States was born from an awareness of its founding fathers that the right of men to freedom is a gift of the creator and that the equality of all can only stem from that gift. "I tremble for my country," said Thomas Jefferson, "when I reflect on the fact that God is just and that His justice cannot sleep forever."[2] Today Jefferson would have far more reason to tremble. The life of Americans has gone astray. Freedom has largely been shorn of its components, commitment, and discipline. For many people justice has become a mockery. The alternatives which are presented to us are false choices. Our survival was never a question of war or peace, disarmament or nuclear death, white or black, poor or rich. What is at stake is the very soul of man, his destiny in the world, the objectives of human society in time and eternity.

People with a limited outlook cannot achieve great ends. The greatness of a nation is not a question of industrial might, military power, or size of its population. The greatness of a nation depends on its objectives and on the character of its leaders and its citizenry. That nation is truly great that finds the answer to the divisions which beset our societies.

Television and radio commentator Rush Limbaugh summarized the first hundred days of the Clinton administration with "gays and taxes." I summarize the American and Western society of today with "lies and bankruptcy."

If America is to pursue its special role in the world as a guiding example and leading power in the service of freedom and justice, millions of Americans must change their objectives and their way of life. The American way of life has to be defined anew. "We have been the recipients of the choicest bounties of Heaven," proclaimed Abraham Lincoln on 30 March 1863.

We have grown in numbers, wealth and power as no other nation has ever grown. But we have forgotten God. We have forgotten the gracious hand which preserved us in peace and multiplied and enriched and strengthened us, and we have vainly imagined, in the deceitfulness of our hearts, that all these blessings were produced by some superior wisdom and virtue of our own. Intoxicated with unbroken success, we have become too self-sufficient to feel the necessity of redeeming and preserving grace, too proud to pray to the God that made us.

It behooves us, then, to humble ourselves before the offended power, to confess our national sins, and to pray for clemency and forgiveness.[3]

This, Americans, is the road to travel, and then the world will follow you.

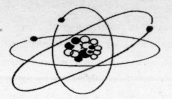

On the Road to Peace?

In September 1991, the president of the United States, George Bush, announced sweeping reductions in the nuclear arsenal of the United States in view of the evolution of democratic forces in the Soviet Union, declaring that we are well ahead on the road to peace and a more secure world. In June 1992, after the dissolution of the Soviet Union, he and Boris Yeltsin met in Washington and signed a treaty with further substantial reductions of nuclear warheads in the United States and Russia. A further treaty was signed in Moscow in January 1993.

Naturally, this is a gratifying development. Instead of adding costly systems to the existing arsenal year after year, we have begun to destroy what we have in our warehouses and to reduce our active military forces, expecting the other side to do the same. I agree that the threat of a surprise military attack on the West is greatly reduced. I am grateful that my country, Germany, has become one nation again, and that Soviet occupation troops have not only left her soil but the countries of our eastern neighbors as well. The economic, ecological, and spiritual destruction they leave behind is another matter. I do not believe that we are progressing towards peace, since I have never considered the threat of Soviet arms as the major obstacle to peace. I always considered our self-destructive way of life more dangerous to peace than the Soviet long-range missiles with nuclear warheads directed to us. The real danger, in my view, lies in the attitudes and philosophies we are allowing to shape our lives,

which make conflict inevitable and lead to the use of arms—
nuclear or non-nuclear. Those attitudes have not changed fundamentally, and we shall continue to live in a dangerous world
with the gears shifting and deadly conflicts surfacing in other
settings. There will be no peace unless we change our philosophies and our ways. Many years ago, the author Vaclav Havel,
now president of the Czech Republic, expressed the same thought:
"The greatest mistake Western Europe could make would be
not to understand totalitarian systems as what in the last instance they are, the vaulted mirror of modern civilization and a
hard—perhaps last call to this civilization for a general revision
of it's understanding of self."[1]

The Marxist-Leninist Concept of Peace

The German philosopher George Wilhelm Friedrich Hegel
stated in the early nineteenth century that all events in the world
were a reflection of the development of the absolute world spirit,
which unfolds by a dialectic process from thesis through antith-
esis to synthesis until, in the last phase, history is fulfilled and
completed when the human spirit understands its own meaning
by reference to the reason inherent in the world. His vague and
complex concepts, when stripped of their philosophical jargon
and reduced to ordinary language, may perhaps be defined as a
worldly embodiment of the Christian concept of the Kingdom
of God. Human existence is defined by Hegel as part of the
historical process, detached from any relationship to a super-
natural God. According to Hegel, the spirit comes first and
matter second.

Marx developed his historical materialism on this foundation. To some extent, he turned Hegel's views upside down by
proclaiming the priority of matter over spirit. Material conditions—the infrastructure—determine spiritual, cultural, social,
and political relationships in human society, he said. As material
and economic conditions develop, so new classes arise which
dispute the dominant position of the existing ruling class. According to Marx, history consists of a sequence of class struggles
culminating automatically in the classless Communist society,
which knows no exploitation of man by other men and in which

all men are equal. Consequently, capitalism—with which communists equate western democracy—is sentenced to death, and it is merely matter of time when the death throes end. Because of its philosophy of class struggle, which sets one group up against the other, Marxism and peace exclude each other.

Lenin changed Marxist historical materialism by enriching the automatic cycle of history with a concept of the use of force by professional revolutionary elites. According to Marx, historical development will automatically culminate in Communist society when the victorious industrial proletariat puts an end to the dominant capitalist class. But in Russia in 1917, the industrial proletariat was not large enough to justify that theory since there was a much larger number of peasants or agricultural serfs. Therefore the Russian social-democratic reformers wanted to postpone the revolution until later when there were enough proletarians. Lenin had no intention to wait and adapted Marxism to the prevailing Russian conditions of that time. He included the agricultural population into the Marxist theory and destroyed the beginning of democracy after the ousting of the Czar by others.

Stalin, in contrast to the Marxist theory of the gradual extinction of the state, replaced Lenin's revolutionaries by bureaucrats who see themselves as the advance guard of the last victorious class of humanity, the proletariat, whose task is to bring history to its fulfillment and fruition.

Gorbachev, with the same sense of historical mission, started out by trying to bring the backward Soviet state into the modern world without giving up his basic philosophy. Events overtook him and developed their own movement. In the whole of the Soviet Union and Eastern Europe, people were just too fed up with Communist lies, brutality, and mismanagement and broke out of the limitations. According to the Russian dissident Vladimir Bukowski, the concept of *perestroika* was not developed by Gorbachev but by the Politburo under KGB Chief and President Yuri Andropov. Suslov, the ideological Soviet "pope," was one of the strategists. Andropov, who was the mentor of Gorbachev and who put him into his position of power, defined his concept of peace in 1982 in Moscow before an elite audience:

Lenin..., the founder of our party, always made a clear
distinction between just and unjust wars. His views on
the problem of war and peace constitute a coherent doc-
trine, the main objective of which is a consistent and
uncompromising assertion of the idea that peace and
socialism are intrinsically connected. This connection stems
from the fact that the new society has no need for war,
that war stands in sharp contradiction to all its interests
and ideals and to all the aspirations of the working people.
Today when the question of war and peace is a life-or-
death matter for whole peoples and for human civilization in general, the relevance of these Leninist ideas has
grown particularly acute.[2]

In other words, the Marxist-Leninist concept of peace is
quite different from ours. It is not the contrary of shooting war,
but rather the rule of Socialism, i.e., communism exercising
global power.

I have read Gorbachev's book *A Time for Peace*, but I could
not find a single thought of any substance. I see that book like
the subsequent one, *Perestroika*, as a refined attempt to delude
the West as to his true intentions. Like Khrushchev before him
he makes no reference to the real battlefields, namely society,
religion, morals and ideology, and speaks instead of interstate
relations—a tactic which can also be detected in the Helsinki
accords and to which the West always fells prey. It became clear
to me as I went through the pages of his peace book that he was
not really seeking peace in our meaning of the word, but advantages.

Therefore, the Marxist-Leninist concept of history, which
aims at the destruction of our values, is still in place and peace-
preventing. There may be a tactical short-term accommodation
but a long-term everlasting ideological war. A Marxist-Leninist
is a person who is embedded in a historical process, whose life
is part of a global struggle for power. The battle for the minds
and hearts of men, which is the battle for peace, goes on unabated.

We are blind to this aspect and, hence, to the world as a
whole since we do not know this dimension to life. This has two
causes. First, modern man has no sense of history and directs all
his energies toward the search for his own happiness here and

now, and nobody, other than the Marxists, offers him an overall world view for whose attainment a personal commitment seems worthwhile. Secondly, we suffer from a moral decadence which has grown up over the centuries and considers the amoral and abnormal as progress. We know that our economic system produces an ever-growing series of new technological developments and prosperity which the Communist system is unable to do. We are convinced that neither ourselves nor the overwhelming majority of the population can be converted to communism. We have not taken communism seriously, because we believe that its spread depends on the number of conversions and the functioning of the economic system. We do not understand the connection between morals and totalitarianism—that immorality, no matter what we call it, is the stepping stone to totalitarian rule. So we feel secure and superior and have treated the Soviet Union as an aggressive military superpower. Now that the threat seems to be gone, we can relax—we think. But the alternatives we see are false. It has never been primarily a question of peace or war, disarmament, or nuclear death. What has been at stake is the very soul of man, his destiny in the world, the objective of human society in time and eternity. It is either God's terms for peace or human self-destruction. A philosophy which blames the ills of society on somebody else cannot lead to peace, only to unending power struggles.

The Western Illusion

Our Western concept of peace in reality means peace for us even though we don't say so. Instead we speak of advancing peace, liberty, and democratic values around the world. Our actions betray our words. We want to be left in peace so as to be able to do as we please—but that is not peace. The American journalist William Pfaff, not inhibited by political constraint, made this point quite clear a few years ago. He stated that the Wall and the division of Germany was a good and necessary state of affairs, because it provided a balance between East and West and stability in an otherwise unstable situation brought about by unstable Germans. He, of course, was thinking of stability for himself and his crowd and not of the human needs of those on the other side of the Wall. He did not aspire for them what I am sure he considers indispensable for himself. His views are symptomatic of Western selfishness because he only expressed what millions of people and innumerous political leaders also thought.

Peace is the opposite of war. The error of most peace seekers is founded in their concept of war, which they see as an armed conflict between two hostile countries or groups. They also tend to believe that the situation today is particularly dangerous because of the existence of nuclear weapons. Peace is therefore understood as the avoidance of an armed conflict, primarily between the great powers. The Carter Center in Atlanta counted at the end of 1992 a total of 112 local wars all over the world—for the most part bloody civil wars. According to experts at the Hamburg University, there were 52 wars in 1992. They point out that the level of violence and armed conflicts in the world is rising constantly. In the fifties, there was an average of 12 wars raging at any time. In the sixties, the average rose to 22, then to 32 in the seventies, and 40 in the eighties. Helped by the incompetent, superficial, and dishonest reporting of our media, we only focus on a few which make the headlines, like the war in former Yugoslavia, and disregard the others because we think most of these wars are of no consequence to us, not related to what we consider as the main threat to our peace: the Soviet government and their nuclear weaponry. However, the global social war today is being fought by different rules than the wars between nation-states in previous centuries and is not necessarily fought with weapons. The front lines run through each parliament, each newspaper editorial room, and each family. This can be clearly observed in the Judiciary Committee of the United States Senate listening to the reasons stated by the fourteen senators for approving or rejecting the nomination of Judge Clarence Thomas to the Supreme Court. The issue was not Thomas and his judicial qualification but the moral and ideological direction of American society.

In the Senate Hearings and later in the full Senate discussions, I could perceive the same sentiment from our period of disgrace in Germany, which will ring in my ears to the end of my years: "If you don't think as we do, you have had it!" Naturally, the "You have had it" means something different in Washington now than what it meant in Nazi Germany at that time. But if you think of the legalized murdering of millions of unborn lives in America today, this difference may shrink over the years to come. If ever anybody wanted a demonstration of the interrelationship between Marxism-Leninism—the means justifying the ends, nazism character assassination to purify the cause, and the destruction of absolute moral values—he had it in front of him. Like in Nazi Germany, it seemed to me that Thomas could not speak out for what he really believed in, because of the negative repercussions it would have had on his nomination. I have seen the same conflict in my father. It was the central issue for millions of Germans, who were not Nazis but were exposed to their ruthlessness. The mobilized hatred and intolerance of organizations and their leaders, who want to enforce their ideas "and stop at nothing," as Judge Thomas expressed it, was a reality then, as it is now. Thomas was prepared to be killed in the process. There is no difference between dying on the battlefield fighting for your country or being crucified for your beliefs. In this case it was "high-tech lynching for uppity blacks," an organized class war, not a race war, at the heart of central democratic procedures. It was obvious who is on what side of the battle line and who are the opportunists bowing to the pressure of the vote. Of course there were honest people on both sides, just having different opinions, but turning one's back on one's own knowledge of what is right in order to appease popular demand. To gain reelection advantages is like raising the white flag to the enemy in a shooting war. America, beware of the direction you are heading.

The polarization of opinions, which can be witnessed in Washington and in every other capital, reflects a dangerous state of affairs. Only the participants have not yet defined it. The Bundestag Defense Committee in Bonn, for years in the eighties, confined itself in the formal committee meetings to the discussion of generalities, while the hard decisions were discussed at unofficial breakfasts in the absence of those the majority of the committee members conceived to be enemies of our free society. The fact that both camps have the same passport and speak the same language is of secondary importance. It is

the hate-filled, envious non-Communist international class fighters and appeasers in the Western governments and parliaments,
who not only have been handing over free people to the knife in
their blind search for peace, but are also destroying the very
foundations in our countries on which peace must be built. And,
those people who were excluded from the defense committee
meetings in Bonn in 1995 have become a recognized part of the
establishment. They have not changed their concepts, but everybody else has moved to the Left—on the road to the Soviet
concept of peace.

World War II was already a social and ideological conflict
cloaked in the garb of nationalism. The Soviet Union was a
military ally of the West in pursuit of its own imperialistic objectives, and at all times a deadly ideological enemy of the Western democracies. Western leaders were too self-absorbed to see
the reality and thought that the so-called Cold War began in
1947 with Churchill's speech in Fulton, Missouri. An ally, so
they thought, had turned into an enemy. But, there was no
transformation. It only became apparent what Lenin had established thirty years earlier and had been Soviet policy ever since.
Until today, I believe, Americans have had two different categories for Stalin—the ally and Stalin, the mass murderer. A kind
of schizophrenia, as though the two people and what they represent were not connected with each other. And, naturally, they
think of Roosevelt as a great president—after all he won the
war—while in reality he was a vain disaster being taken for a ride
by his friend, Joe Stalin.

The Nazi Road, Lies and License

Hitler was a master of psychological warfare, as the English
military historian Liddel Hart explained. He had understood
better than any general how bloodless conquests, which pre-
ceded war as such, could be brought about by undermining the
will to resist. Mao conquered Chiang Kai-chek's Nationalist
China by applying the same concept—and of course, with the
help of the West.

Nobody took the trouble to compare Hitler's categorical
declarations of his intention to go to war put down unequivo-

cally in his book *Mein Kampf*, with his later speeches in which he expressed his quest for peace. He lied for tactical reasons, and his lies were all too readily accepted by Western leaders as the expression of his political strategy, because that was infinitely more comfortable and required no active response. Hitler's affirmations of his commitment to peace were made for purely propaganda purposes: "Necessity was the reason for which I spoke only of peace for many years . . . it then became imperative to gradually change German thinking and make the German people realize that there are things which must be attained by force if they cannot be achieved by peaceful means,"[3] were his words on 10 November 1938.

Land for Peace

On 30 September 1938, Hitler and Neville Chamberlain signed a declaration, which ended: "We are resolved to deal with other questions concerning both our countries by the method of consultation and to make further endeavors to remove the possible causes of differences of opinion so as to contribute in this way to safeguarding peace in Europe."[3] The French Prime-Minister Daladier added:

> I believe that the Munich agreement may constitute a historic date in the life of Europe. Thanks to the high degree of understanding shown by the representatives of the great powers, war has been avoided and an honorable peace ensured between all the people. I had the pleasure of ascertaining for myself that there are no feelings of hatred or hostility in Germany. You may rest assured that for their part the French feel no hostility whatever towards Germany. This also holds good in the periods of diplomatic tensions and military preparations which we have experienced. Our two people must understand each other fully and I am happy to devote my strength to the promotion of this necessary and fruitful understanding. I have already thanked the Führer, Marshal Goering and the Reich foreign minister, von Ribbentrop, for their cordial welcome . . .[4]

It was only later that these three gangsters came to be described as war criminals. When appeasers make deals with gangsters, no peace can come out of it. They gave land—other peoples' land—for peace and reaped war.

Chamberlain and Daladier wanted peace for their countries but not peace and justice for others, including Czechs, Slovaks, and Germans. Their expectations were not related to the reality of the world at that time because of their wishful thinking. They were talking to an evil ruler, not to another people. They equated the people with their masters, so there was no peace—only war.

We continue our quest for peace on the basis of the same illusions. The two Western leaders did not have at that time such an accomplished vision of the importance of the organization of the economy as our leaders have today. The totalitarian threat from Hitler had nothing to do with economy. Germany had a booming free-market economy and was still considered by Roosevelt and Churchill to be more dangerous than the Soviet Union under Stalin with its centrally controlled economy. If economy had no bearing on the totalitarian bid for world power then, why should it today?

The Middle East Mess

Are we today any closer to peace in the Middle East? Did our war with Iraq result in more justice for the people of Iraq and of the region? Has the Baker—and consequent Warren Christopher—shuttle diplomacy been a chance for a lasting peace accord between the Israeli and Arab people? I have more the impression that the wrong Arabs with the help of the United States are ganging up on Israel. I think it is plain stupid to try to organize peace without addressing hatred. Time will show. Many things may have happened before this book was printed. But I have little doubt that again we have embarked on the wrong road to peace. Let us look at the record.

First we drop the shah because he doesn't come up to our demanding standard of human rights. It does not take us very long to discover that the Ayatollah Khomeini is even worse. We therefore associate ourselves with Saddam Hussein, "to keep a stable balance of power" and order in the area. It is the Western nations who made this monster into the menace of the world he then became. He was known to be an assassin for a long time, but for the sake of order and stability we overlooked that fact. In 1979 he had condemned six members of his cabinet to death, because he considered their loyalty to him questionable, and had the rest of the cabinet execute them in a firing squad. A few years later, he shot another minister in front of the cabinet. Amnesty International reported in 1989 that hundreds of children were tortured and murdered in order to silence dissenting parents. When he went after the Kurds using poisonous gas against the civilian population and subjugated them with his murderous brutality, the world community kept silent and did not lift a finger. The United Nations considered the slaughter an internal matter of Iraq since the twenty million Kurds are not represented in this international organization. I do not understand how later on the United Nations and the Western hypocrites found their moral indignation, when the Kuwaitis, much less in numbers, got into the firing line. Of course, they have oil and the Kurds do not.

Being an ally, Saddam Hussein was also a much desired client. Everybody wanted to do business with him and assured him that he was well respected. The Germans installed the chemical and industrial capacity enabling him to produce poisonous gas, pretending not to know what it was for. The French provided 20 percent of all his weapons including Mirage F-1 fighter planes along with Roland and Exocet missiles; Italy delivered nuclear technology. The U.S. provided helicopters and computers. The Soviets provided 50 percent of Iraq's armament, most of it during the years of peace-loving Gorbachev. Ten billion dollars of the total bill of $23.5 billion are not yet paid— so Gorbachev asked the West for financial help to maintain his shaky empire. There are other countries like Brazil, South Africa, China, Belgium, and Egypt, to name only a few, which eagerly contributed to strengthening the Iraqi regime in return for money.

Then Saddam Hussein invaded Kuwait. All of a sudden he was declared to be the most evil dictator in the world, comparable only to Hitler, which I think is a fair description. We went to war and blamed Saddam Hussein to be responsible for it. He certainly is an aggressor and needed to be stopped, but we in the

West were responsible for the war because of our immoral appeasement of an evil government and our greed to make money with him. Therefore we were not fighting a war because of somebody else, but were dealing simply with the consequences of our rotten, peace-destroying and war-producing attitudes and behavior, which we refuse to face and do not want to call by their proper name. It is we who made war inevitable. "We tried to bring Iraq into the family of nations, but we were not successful," said both George Bush and James Baker later, trying to justify their handling of the prewar situation—as though evil could be made less evil by appeasement.

We Westerners may accuse other countries of human rights violations if they torture people and murder them, but what about our policy of systematic violation and destruction of the aspirations of whole nations whose immoral rulers we collaborate? What about President Mitterand of France and his state-owned armament industry selling weapons to Iraq for them to be used against his own soldiers? The French always sold weapons to anybody, regardless of their ideological color or human rights record—to the Sandinistas as well as to the Angolan allies of Fidel Castro. Shouldn't Mitterand be brought to trial for collaboration with a criminal government instead of some Kuwaiti collaborators who tried to save their necks? And what about Nobel Peace Prize acrobat Gorbachev? The indiscriminate collaboration of democratic leaders with totalitarian governments constitutes the most serious violation of human rights, and until that fact is being faced and dealt with, especially in the United Nations, there will be no peace in the world.

The Gulf War cost $60 billion which could have been better spent in Eastern Europe or Latin America, if we would have applied moral principles from the beginning. We win the shooting war in great style and leave the murderous Saddam Hussein in place, forget about his similarities with Hitler and treat him again as a legitimate head of state. We excuse ourselves by saying that there was no mandate from the United Nations, but since when does a faceless body of bureaucrats decide about peace and war? Saddam Hussein immediately turned with all his brutality on the opposition within his own country, the Kurds and Shiits, and crushed them with the weapons we should have taken from him. Representatives of the Kurds said on 8 April 1991 before the National Press Club in Washington, that in the twenty-four hours after President Bush's order to stop the fighting, eighteen hundred tanks, twenty-four hundred armored vehicles, and three divisions of the Republican Guard escaped the Kuwaiti encirclement. Allowing them to leave cost tens of thousands of Kurds and Shiits their lives and brought further destruction on Iraq. We may thank God for getting us out of the war with so few casualties, but I consider this pure unchristian hypocrisy and doubt that such a prayer sounds acceptable in the ears of the Lord. It is not true that our Western lives are more valuable than the lives of other people. Does the commandment to be the guardian of your brother not apply to a government? The Kuwaiti and Saudi rulers, who financed Saddam Hussein and other terrorists for years to buy themselves peace, regardless of the suffering of others, did not lift a finger to help the Kurds. They cried for justice when they got into the firing line, and in my view do not merit the blood of any soldier of the allied forces. They benefited from the need to stop an aggressor. However, in the end we did not win a victory for peace and justice, but contributed to an increase in the suffering of millions. What precisely did we try to achieve? Put an undemocratic, womanizing autocrat back into office? Stop aggression and then let a new one get on the way?

The war effort will not bring peace. On the contrary, the level of desperation, misery, and hatred is rising. While United Nations teams look for the Scud missiles and their bases in Iraq in order to destroy them, Syria announced it is going to produce them in a joint venture with Iran. Iran is buying up weaponry from Russia at the tune of $2 billion a year, including nuclear technology; that, though, does not prevent our Western statesmen from giving Russia a financial package of $100 billion without prohibiting such arms sales. As soon as Saddam Hussein transformed himself from an ally and client into an enemy, we turned immediately to Hafez Assad, president of Syria, to ally ourselves with him in order to orchestrate a new infrastructure of stability through a balance of power in the region and check the threat this time, not of Khomeni, but of Saddam Hussein. Syria is classified by the State Department as a terrorist country and Assad is the same ruthless criminal and oppressor as Saddam Hussein. We do the same kind of thing to the Syrian people what we have done to the Iraqi people, leave them to the mercy of a gangster. Whoever has been at the Golan Heights, and I was there, cannot but conclude that the government of Israel would be suicidal to deliver those strategic hills which dominate the wide plateau of Galilei to a terrorist like Hafez Assad. Syria as a democratic and nonaggressive country would be quite another matter, but at this point it does not exist. There is no way to get anywhere close to peace unless there is a fundamental change of attitudes and government structures in the region. Hatred and indifference must be transformed into caring for and respecting others. Nothing of this sort is happening. The issue is not even addressed. The concept (land for peace) is complete nonsense and as unreal as the Munich Accord of 1938 by which Hitler got land and kept the peace for eleven months.

Therefore, I think Baker's and Christopher's efforts are a waste of time and money because their concept of peace is limited. It is in line with the record of peace treaties, by which order is imposed on one group by another, in order to get rid of some problem in the short run. And why was the Soviet Union invited at that time to participate in the so-called peace process? Why should a faraway government of a country whose ruling party had seventy years history of repression, murder, and incompetence, and was at that time already at the brink of bankruptcy have any say in the affairs of other countries? It is naive. It is also plain stupid and very dangerous.

It becomes apparent that we are not dealing here with a one-time mistake, a mistaken concept for lack of adequate information, or a wrong judgment related to a specific situation with specific people. Rather, we are dealing with a pattern of political mismanagement, a system of errors which is being repeated year after year, decade after decade, in situation after situation, by one Western government after the other. In this particular case, the Western action was led by the U.S. secretary of state, James Baker. I am not speaking, however, just about him, but see him as representative of basic Western foreign policy principles, wrong from beginning to the end, applied by all our governments, including my own.

The example of the divided Germany may help to make my point clear. The West German government sincerely wanted to help our compatriots in East Germany and tried for decades to find a relationship with the Communist government. Hundreds of billions of marks were disbursed in one way or another to the slave masters in East Berlin with the purpose of improving the lives of the East Germans. When the Wall finally came down, what did we find? Where was the improvement our money was supposed to have produced? We found a bankrupt economy, a destroyed ecology, and people worse off than at the beginning of Communist rule. Our money was used to cement the apparatus of oppression and to finance the lifestyle of some hundred thousand nomenclatura apparatchiks and their subversive actions around the world. When Honecker was exchanged in 1989 for Egon Krenz as head of the East German state and the Communist party, West German president, Richard von Weizsaecker, congratulated him by cable on his election, disregarding the fact that Krenz was elected by a small group of functionaries in the totalitarian politburo and that millions of East Germans were already demonstrating in the streets against the very same politburo. I have talked to various high-ranking West German government officials and I do not doubt their sincerity, but from the president down to the last citizen, nobody had a moral ideological concept to overcome the lie of communism with the truth of God and beat them at their own game. Instead we legitimized the rulers in the eyes of the oppressed. And now we have to pour in hundreds of billions more to repair the devastation. That in turn, considering the consequent high interest situation, had a negative effect on the whole of the world economy.

Even though it is true that each situation is different from the other and has to be handled according to its own merit, there has to be a universal concept for government action—a criteria and set of principles which are applied to all situations by all players. That simply does not exist; therefore each government sets its own relative standards and kind of muddles through.

Cheating is wrong in this situation but very necessary in another, so to speak.

Western governments ally themselves with immoral partners whose lack of ethics, or even criminal record, they disregard. They make a plan which they think serves them best according to their criteria and interests of the moment, and then try to push, blackmail, or order others into compliance with that plan. The whole thing is called a peace process, because peace is what is expected to appear at the end of the efforts. Frontiers are being drawn up, alliances organized, convenient governments installed, and people are being moved accordingly. This was the way the African countries of today were created; how the present Middle East mess was started; how the eastern, central, and southeastern Europe including Yugoslavia were divided up; and the same principle is also applied all over Asia. Human suffering, a precondition for war and not for peace, is the inevitable result. The war may not directly involve us, but it will surely have a negative impact on the area we meddle in. And, in one way or another, it gets back to us, if only in the form of costly expenses. The ethnic divisions and the fighting, which we see popping up in Eastern and southeastern Europe, are an expression of this. People have been herded into state units, where they don't belong and do not want to be. The criteria at the creation was power, narrow national and security self-interest, instead of self-determination and justice for other people. We appease the strong and push the weak; when things get very bad, humanitarian aid gets on the way. As a rule, ethnic unrest is the consequence of a majority not respecting minorities—one faction placing their own selfish interests before the rights of others. In eastern Europe, for instance, various groupings—Germans, Poles, Russians, Ukrainians, Lithuanians, Hungarians, Rumanians, Czechs, Serbs, Croats and many others—have been a cruel majority as well as a suffering minority at some time. Therefore, they don't need others to tell them what to do and force frontiers upon them, but they may need help to overcome themselves and their own selfishness. They need a philosophy of life that is valid for all people in order to find lasting solutions. And that, we don't have, and therefore we can't give.

The principle of self-interest, which is not the same as personal and national interests, is based on the desire to find solutions which serve us. Basically it is national selfishness and self-centeredness which dominates foreign policy. That leads to appeasement of evil as long as, in our view, it poses little or no threat to ourselves in a given situation. To achieve our national objectives and safeguard our own existence, we accept other governments as partners, whose ethical standards we recognize to be inadequate or nonexistent. In other words, we compromise with evil to achieve our own peace and leave subjugated people at the mercy of their rulers who we ally with. We have elevated this principle to normal policy because, otherwise, our politicians and the experts in Western foreign ministries would be highly frustrated because they would not know how to achieve anything. "Politics and morals are incompatible." So it goes, not just with regards to foreign policy but to all politics. Wrong! Because of this concept constantly being applied we have created one mess after another and get further and further away from lasting peace. Additionally, foreign ministers get blind to what evil is since they get accustomed to their alliances and deals, which sometimes are even labeled as statesmanship. Western political opportunism based on disguised selfishness is as incompatible to peace as is the Marxist-Leninist philosophy. Eastern and Western materialism alike lead into the same blind alley. National security and peace are not safeguarded by shortsighted deals but by justice for all the people concerned.

Peace Through Change of Heart

Peace means the living together in harmony by people and as well by nations. It is not the framework but the attitudes which are decisive. People can live in the same house but hate and fight each other bitterly; this is war, even if there are no weapons. Anything which produces division between people and nations is anti-peace. Every conflict between self-seeking parties weakens the quest for peace. The fundamental issue in a given conflict is the goal sought by the parties involved, whether they are looking merely for their own advantage or for justice.

The person and the party who seeks justice will find solutions. Our objectives are decided in our hearts and it is completely immaterial whether the heart beats behind black, yellow, brown, or white skin; in a poor or rich, northern or southern environment; in a Catholic or Protestant, Islamic or Buddhist scheme of things. Love and hatred, indifference or sensitivity have the same roots in the human heart. Man and his innermost feelings are therefore the decisive battlefield of the social conflict of today in the quest for peace. Progress should not be measured by economic parameters only, but by the extent which each member of a society and societies as a whole are able to rise above their own self-seeking motives and pursue true justice.

"There can be no lasting peace which permits men to indulge their own personal pleasures and fight their own private wars," said Frank Buchman, founder of Moral Rearmament, in a radio speech on 29 October 1939. "Peace is not an idea, but people becoming different," he added. "Most of us want to make peace by repenting the sins of others."[5] The German Protestant Church Conference in Frankfurt in 1987 was full of such repenting souls, like the girl who prayed for forgiveness of the sins of the bankers, the young man who regretted the German attack on the Soviet Union, and the many hypocrites who recognized the sins of the Boers against their black compatriots, but made no mention of the treatment of unwanted foreigners in Germany.

I have experienced Buchman's concept that change must not begin with others but in each individual himself as the most creative attitude in society and in working with other men. His concept involves a challenge to lead one's own life as one would expect others to do. Very few people think of anything so simple. Hardly anyone relates peace to his own life or our present social chaos to his own outlook and lifestyle. The individual sees his own good intentions and the atrocious deeds of others: "What can little me do? What difference do my actions make?" Thus responsibility is passed on to others, whose impossible behavior is seen as the principal reason for the unsatisfactory situations which prevail.

Change and peace are expected to result from external events, while peace in the true sense of the word can only come from within, from our personal existence. This naturally may lead to conferences and disarmament as a consequence. Only people who live at peace with themselves can create peace for others. Hypocrites, adulterers, thieves, liars, homosexuals, and the power-hungry who do not seek justice but power for themselves cannot bring peace but destruction to human society. The individual who remains neutral in the face of evil and wrongs others, and the person or nation who remains indifferent to suffering and poverty is gnawing at the very foundation of peace. Governments which live in a state of war with their own people are incapable of peace. Societies in which people are at war with each other are an obstacle to peace.

"The lives of men must change if the problems are to be solved. Peace in the world can stem only from peace in the heart of man,"[6] said Frank Buchman in Geneva in 1932. According to the German philosopher Karl Jaspers, "to bring about a change in the world it is admittedly not enough for each individual to change himself. But that is a prerequisite for the change to a new policy in which wars will cease."[7]

Centuries earlier, Thomas-a-Kempis expressed the same view in the following terms:

> First maintain peace and order in yourself and then you will be able to bring about peace and order in others. A man who bears peace within him is more useful than one who has a vast body of learning; the man who is blown to and fro by violent passions tends to destroy all that is good and places his faith in that which is bad. But the peace lover directs everything towards the best conclusion. He who lives at peace with himself thinks ill of no one. But he who lives at war with himself will soon be blown hither and thither by all kinds of folly. He knows no peace and leaves none for others. He often says what he should not have said and does not what he should have done. He looks only at that which others should do and fails to do what he should have done. Let therefore your zealous action begin with yourself; only then may it justifiably be transferred to your neighbours.[8]

"For the Godless are like a raging sea that cannot come to rest and whose waters are full of mud and dirt," said Isaiah. "For the Godless there is no peace, thus saith the Lord" (Isa. 57:21).

Peace is as indivisible as freedom. Peace is not an end in itself. Peace is the fruit of justice for all men and people brought about by men and women without resentment and hatred who live at peace with themselves and care for others and for other nations. Those who look for peace and not for justice will get nowhere. Those who fight for justice for others will find peace.

Stronger than the winds of freedom and democracy which are blowing over the world is the storm of hatred and misery which is gaining hurricane force. Whatever disarmament agreements and armistices may be signed, whatever limitations may be imposed on immigration, the storm flood of human flotsam will spread across the frontiers of those countries which are better off. The starving of millions of people will accelerate the hurricane force regardless of whatever humanitarian aid is administered.

The seed of hatred and self-seeking will grow horrifyingly in our Western society unless we change. Social justice and compassion cannot be legislated on the basis of indebting future generations, but our concepts must encompass the poorest of this world whose right to live as human beings is our responsibility. It does not matter that there are national frontiers between us. If we live straight there will be no lack of means. Western society needs to look outward and not inward. We need broader horizons, a revolution in our hearts and minds in which the destructive Marxist and the selfish bourgeois nationalistic intellectual structures will be broken down, so that a new way of thinking, living, and acting can bring about a new world order in which peace will reign.

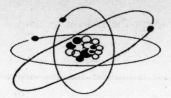

The Ultimate Purpose of History

For the first time in history, mankind truly has the potential to wreak destruction. But this threat appears far less terrifying when we consider the millions of human beings now living on our earth who are in effect no more than walking corpses. They have the appearance of human beings and seem to be alive, but they have killed the spirit of truth within themselves and will one day be called to account for it. It is people with the wrong way of life which constitute the greatest threat to humanity. Czeck statesman and writer Václav Havel long before the Wall came down had pointed out, that the greater threat to Western civilization was itself rather than from SS-20 rockets.

Also for the first time in history, the notion that all men are equal has gained general acceptance, although the attainment of this ideal still seems remote as ever. Modern techniques of communication have enabled links to be established between all mankind. For the first time then, the prerequisites exist for the creation of a world society of free and equal sovereign nations.

Limitations, on thought patterns and intellectual structures from which even the finest of our ancestors could not escape, have disappeared. The Bill of Rights, which marked the inception of democratic development in the West, did not apply in its day to everyone but only to the nobility.

Martin Luther believed that a man's religion was the overriding factor. In his eyes, the Jews were simply a people who had denied Jesus; he did not recognize their specific culture and role in history. Thomas Jefferson saw nothing wrong with slavery, and his contemporaries did not accept the Indians as normal human beings.

Today we know that all men are equal, regardless of their race, religion or social origin, but we fail to put that knowledge into practice, one reason being that the term *equal* is often confused with *identical*. We have not yet achieved an overall view of man, society, and the world and we are following erroneous doctrines which do not unite but rather set apart, and are having catastrophic economic and political consequences.

Leaders of the developing countries, such as Julius Nyere, to name but one, who believed that they had started on the road to independence, found themselves and their countries in a state of even greater dependence than before. They failed to take seriously the truth of the Hindu religion enshrined in the Bhagavadgita which says that real independence can only come from the renunciation of the crippling, base forces within the human personality. The decisive factor is not race or class but the quality of individual life. False political tenets stem from a wrong attitude of life. Nothing that lasts can grow on the barren soil of envy. Self-seeking is an uninspired way of life in that all the supposed intermediate tenets to which men may subscribe between "capitalism" and "socialism" lead to the same dead end.

Change must begin with each individual, not with others but with each man himself. "Everybody has to begin with himself," explains Václav Havel. "Would one wait for the other all would wait in vain."[1]

He who follows truth within himself will find true freedom. There can be no freedom without truth; democracy cannot function with liars. "Blessed are the ears which do not heed the voice from without, but only listen to the truth within,"[2] said Thomas a Kempis.

David Ben-Gurion named his son Amos after the prophet Amos, who believed that God was not only the God of Israel but the God of all men everywhere. Ben-Gurion told his wife Paula that, according to Amos, God would punish those who treat the poor cruelly. He recalled the words of the prophet according to whom the children of Israel would one day return to their land, and live in peace and prosperity.

Half of that prophecy has been fulfilled. Peace will ensue not because of the activities of the Warren Christophers, but when the people of Israel and their government will follow the path of Moses: obedience to their master. The hatred, which drives the Arab hypocrites who claim to follow the teaching of Mohammed while disregarding the fact that love of a man's neighbor is an integral part of that same teaching, is a reality but not an insurmountable obstacle. Israel can still fulfill its historic mission, if its government sets out to listen to God's will and obeys as Moses did.

The Islamic Arabs, whose contemporary contribution to the development of the family of man has so far consisted of charging horrendous oil prices to developing countries and in exporting assassination to the airways and on land all over the world, should first put an end to murderous state terror. They could in reality change the world if they replaced their cruelty, intolerance, and indifference by a sense of responsibility towards their fellow men of all creeds.

In our world today, the decisive struggle is the struggle for power which seemed only superficially to take the shape of a conflict between the super powers. That is why the notion of a Cold War, which we claim to have won, fails to address the underlying reality. The true issue is the nature of the force which is to rule those men who wield power. There are only two alternatives for mankind: The rule of God through men guided by Him or the rule of almighty man. One of the two will win the day; it will be life or death, and history is moving closer to the moment of decision.

The base of Marxist philosophy is to blame somebody else. That concept was systematically built into every aspect of Socialist society and the repulsion of the enemy is a constant feature to keep people motivated to serve the state. The focus in society was shifted from responsibility of self to the blame of others. A tendency of human nature, which can be found in each individual, became the law of society. We in the West looked above all indignantly at the consequent Communist aggressiveness without directing ourselves at the underlying base philosophy which needed (and still needs) to be cured on the level of the individual as well as on the level of society.

A closer look at our own society shows that we are not so far away from Marxism as we may think. We only have focussed on a partial aspect of it, the economy. The principle thought of blaming somebody else has been well established in most Western countries. Because if it is true that other people, society, injustices, or whatever are to blame for our unsatisfactory condition, then that means that people are turned into victims, victimized by somebody or something, and need to be compensated by society. And if you listen to the speeches of politicians who want to be reelected around the world, then it becomes clear that we are told precisely that. The result is an ever-growing bureaucracy and the inflation that goes with it.

Such is the purpose and aim of our individual life: to become Christ-like in the control of ourselves and in our love for others, in an active commitment to satisfying the needs of our neighbors and of the less fortunate. Love is the answer to hatred and an abundance of love will change the world. Societies must, by the same token, look outward—not inward, as is the case now. The purpose of government is not just to administer the affairs of their own nation or group of nations but to fight for universal justice on the basis of the same standards for all—for the weak as well as for the strong—in the same way as God's justice is the same for all people. The same principle must be applied in the policy towards their own population as towards all other nations. Because of our godless opportunism, we got into the mess most nations are in—the debts, the inflation, the divisions, the unemployment, venereal diseases, destroyed families, pregnant schoolgirls, rampant crime, poverty, famine, and so forth. It can be changed and then all else will follow. And we shall be surprised. It is the Marxist, the one who blames others and has the illusion that he himself is good, who asks the dumb question, how can God permit a thing like this? and continues to do as he pleases. The one who has accepted responsibility for himself takes up his cross and goes out to fight for change.

There is no permanence in life. All is in a state of flux. Our society and the entire world are moving towards a new era. The sum of scientific knowledge doubles every ten years. New technologies are emerging with bewildering speed. The range of possible progress for mankind is assuming an inconceivable scale. But there is no such thing as an independent historical process. History is made by active men and women, by each one of us. There are only two possible camps in the world: the servants of God and His enemies. Let each man consider to which he wishes to belong. Neutrality does not exist. The lukewarm will be spit out. "Al haqq yalu," say the Arabs: "Truth will conquer."

God's commandments are not a recommendation for the behavior of the individual; they are laws, with which compliance is the only feasible way for mankind to face its future. These are the most important instructions for every president, member of government, senator, congressman, judge, and indeed for each one of us: "I am the Lord your God. You must not have other Gods before me. Honor your father and mother. Do not covet your neighbor's possessions. You must not steal. You must not kill. You must not fornicate. You must not bear false witness." It is easy to understand what we should do, but hard to put that knowledge into practice: "Love your neighbor as you love yourself" (Matt. 7:12).

These commandments must be made the norm of our society in order to change the course of world events. People of the truth must get on the offensive and banish lies from power, from parliaments, the media, and from every aspect of our lives. That is the only way in which swords can be beaten into plowshares.

Thy will be done on earth as it is in heaven.

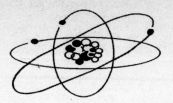

Notes

Chapter 1—Objectives

1. Arkady N. Shevchenko, *Breaking with Moscow* (New York: Alfred Knopf, 1985), 279.

2. Ralph G. Martin, *A Hero for Our Time* (New York: Ballantine Books, 1983), 277.

Chapter 2—Lies

1. Martin Kriele, *Nicaragua—Das blutende Herz Amerikas* (Mürchen: Piper Verlag, 1986), 130.

2. Ibid., 172.

3. Vaclav Havel, *Versuch in der Wahrheit zu leben* (Reinbeck: Rowohlt Verlag, 1990), 17.

4. Alexander Solzhenitsyn, *From under the Rubble* (Boston: Little Brown and Company, 1974), 25.

5. Ibid., 274.

6. Karl Jaspers, *Die Atombombe und die Zukunft des Menschen* (München: R. Piper & Co., 1958), 161.

7. Ibid., 160.

8. Vaclav Havel, *Am Anfang war das Wort* (Reinbeck: Rowohlt Verlag, 1990): 96, 106.

9. "The News" (Mexico City, 21 November 1987).

Chapter 3—Money

1. Ken Auleta, *Greed and Glory in Wall Street* (New York: Warner Books, 1974), 249.

2. Ibid., 108.

3. Ibid., 10.

4. Adams James Ring, *The Big Fix—Inside the S & L Scandal* (New York: John Wiley & Sons, 1990), 51.

5. Ibid., 38.

Chapter 4—The Not-So-Dead Communism

1. Manfred Schell and Werner Kalinka, *Stasi und kein Ende* (Frankfurt/Berlin: Die Welt Ullstein Verlag, 1991), 377.

2. Armando Valladares, *Against All Hope* (New York: Alfred Knopf, 1986), 250.

3. Earl E.T. Smith, *The Fourth Floor* (Washington: Selous Foundation Press, 1990), 227-28.

4. Joseph D. Douglass Jr., *Red Cocaine—The Drugging of America* (Atlanta: Clarion House, 1990), 120.

5. Ibid., 36.

6. Ibid., 180.

7. John Barron, *KGB* (Bern-München: Knaur, 1974), 92.

8. Ibid., 20.

Chapter 5—The Struggle for Chile

1. Eudocio Ravines, *The Yennan Way* (New York: Scribner's Sons, 1951), 10.

2. Ibid., 150.

3. Ibid., 151.

4. Ibid., 152.

5. Ibid., 152, 156.

6. Ibid., 161.

7. Ibid., 175.

8. Ibid., 176.

9. Ibid., 180.

Chapter 7—Communists Take Over South Africa

1. The 20th Anniversary Conference of the IFP—"Whither South Africa?" presidential address by Mangosuthu Buthelezi, MP, Ulundi, 22 July 1995, 6.

2. "Aida Parker" newsletter, Johannesburg, no. 171, January/February 1994.

3. Organization Trends, Johannesburg, December 1993, 3–4.

4. UCANEWS, Johannesburg, Edition 2/94.

5. African National Congress National Consultative Conference June 1985—Commission on Cadre Policy, Political and Ideological Work, Internal Commission Report, Commission on Strategy and Tactics, 17.

6. The 20th Anniversary Conference of the IFP—"Whither South Africa." Presidential Address by Mangosuthu Buthelezi, MP, Ulundi 22 July 1995, 34, 14.

7. Mangosuthu G. Buthelezi, *South Africa My Vision for the Future* (New York: St. Martin's Press, 1990), 10.

8. Ibid., 119.

9. *The New International, A Journal for Marxist Politics and Theory*, vol. 2, no. 2, fall edition (New York, 1985) 71.

10. Ibid., 60.

11. Buthelezi, 112.

12. Ibid., 110.

13. Executive Intelligence Report, *Tiny Towland, The Ugly Face of Neocolonialism in Africa* (Washington, D.C.: Executive Intelligence Review, 1993), 104.

14. The 20th Anniversary Conference of the IFP, 10.

15. Southern Africa Update, vol. 3, no. 8, September 1995.

Chapter 8—The New World Order Hoax

1. Ernst von Hippel, *Mechanisches and Moralisches Rechtsdenken* (Meisenheim: Anton Hain Verlag, 1959), 1.

Chapter 9—The Democratic-Bureaucratic Establishment

1. Boris Yeltsin, "Aufzeichnungen eines Unbequemen," (München: Droemer Knaur, 1990), 193

2. Ibid., 201.

3. Ibid., 201-2.

4. Graham Hanccock, *Lords of Poverty* (New York: The Atlantic Monthly Press, 1989), 93.

5. Ibid., 94.

6. Ibid., 96.

7. Ibid., 99.

8. Ibid., 192-93.

9. Hans Urs Balthasar, *Augustinus der Gottesstaat* (Einsiedeln: Johannes Verlag, 1961), 115.

10. Ibid.

11. Karl Jaspers, *Die Atombombe und die Zukunft des Menschen* (München: R. Piper & Co., 1958), 424.

Chapter 10—Western Society

1. Allan Bloom, *The Closing of the American Mind* (New York: Simon & Schuster, 1987), 64.

2. Thomas Jefferson, "Notes on Virginia," quoted by Francis Bradley in "The American Proposition," (New York: Moral Rearmament, 1977), 79.

3. Abraham Lincoln, Done at the city of Washington, this 30th day of March A.D. 1863, and of the Independence of the United States the eighty-seventh.

Chapter 11—On the Road to Peace?

1. Vaclav Havel, *Am Anfang war das Wort* (Reinbeck: Rowohlt Verlag, 1990), 96.

2. Martin Ebon, *The Andropov File* (New York: McGraw Hill, 1983), 233-4.

3. Werner Maser, *Adolf Hitler Mein Kampf* (Esslingen: Bechtle Verlag, 1981), 222.

4. Völkischer Beobachter, Berlin, 1 October 1938.

5. Frank Buchman, "Für eine Neue Welt" (Bern: Caux Verlag, 1961), 143-4.

6. Ibid., 27.

7. Karl Jaspers, *Die Atombombe und die Zukunft des Menschen* (München: R. Piper & Co., 1958), 470.

8. Thomas-a-Kempis, *Die Nachfolge Christi* (Stuttgart: Reclam, 1954), 67.

Chapter 12—The Ultimate Purpose of History

1. Vaclav Havel, *Am Anfang war das Wort* (Reinbeck: Rowohlt Verlag, 1990), 166.

2. Tomas-a-Kempis, *Die Nachfolge Christi* (Stuttgart: Reclam, 1954), 92.

Also by Hilmar von Campe:

Connecting with the Power of God

What motivates the individual American and his government—God or money? Author Hilmar von Campe grew up in pre-war Germany, thinking that because he went to church he was therefore a Christian. In *Connecting with the Power of God*, von Campe tells his fascinating story as a German, a World War II veteran, and an international businessman.

Whatever he describes—his adventurous escape from a prisoner-of-war camp in Yugoslavia (crossing seven borders to get home in 1945), the philosophy course of his daughter at the University of Boulder, the visit to a Baptist college in Florida in 1994, or the trial of Jesus by Pilate and the Jewish establishment of that time—the perspective from which he views people and situations is surprising and thought-provoking.

Connecting with the Power of God is a call to America to fulfill her true destiny in the world, to be a lighthouse for other nations, and to be truly a nation under God for a new world order—not under the United Nations, but under God.

Connecting with the Power of God is available from:
Dandridge Hall Press, Inc.
P.O. Box 31655 • Lafayette, LA 70593